I0436882

TO RUSSIA
WITH HOPE

by

Eugene N. Crone, Ph.D., CAP, MAC, NCACII, ICADC.

To Russia With Hope

by

Eugene N. Crone, Ph.D., MAC, CAP.

Bloomington, IN  Milton Keynes, UK

authorHOUSE®

AuthorHouse™
1663 Liberty Drive, Suite 200
Bloomington, IN 47403
www.authorhouse.com
Phone: 1-800-839-8640

AuthorHouse™ UK Ltd.
500 Avebury Boulevard
Central Milton Keynes, MK9 2BE
www.authorhouse.co.uk
Phone: 08001974150

© 2006 Eugene N. Crone, Ph.D., MAC, CAP.. All rights reserved.

No part of this book may be reproduced, stored in a retrieval system, or transmitted by any means without the written permission of the author.

First published by AuthorHouse 8/24/2006

ISBN: 1-4259-5613-0 (sc)
ISBN: 1-4259-5612-2 (dj)

Library of Congress Control Number: 2006907236

Printed in the United States of America
Bloomington, Indiana

This book is printed on acid-free paper.

"If you do not understand my silence, you
will not understand my words."
Anonymous

DEDICATION

Look everywhere with your eyes, but with your soul never look at many things, but at one. (V.V. Rozinor)

For Deaf persons, Deafness is a treasure – it's a community, a culture, a lifestyle, a unique way of experiencing the world. Mental health treatment for Deaf persons must take place in an environment that offers an understanding of their language and culture and a knowledge of the implications for treatment of persons with alcohol and drug addictions, as well as mental illness.

Therefore, this book is dedicated to, the National Deaf Academy (NDA) and the numerous Fledgling organizations that have served the population of Deaf alcoholics and addicts. Through Its many experiences, strengths and hope of individuals served by the staff and administrators, They provide the foundation of knowledge conveyed herein.

TRIBUTE

Dr. Carol Goodman was the co-author of our book, "THEY HEAR THROUGH THEIR EYES." She contributes her writings and her vast knowledge of Interpreting for the Deaf and hard of Hearing in the second part of this book "TO RUSSIA WITH HOPE." THE second part is titled: "TREATMENT MODALITIES IN THE UNITED STATES FOR THE DEAF AND HARD OF HEARING." She is the inspiration and the epitome of seeking and nurturing the Spiritual Soul of The Deaf Alcoholic/Addict interpreting their desperate messages of fear and anger to one in the Present of love and hope. In the many workshops at conventions and conferences we have Presented, Carol is an inspiration in her messages of faith to the program of recovery for Deaf People. She writes from her heart and her great knowledge as an Interpreter and Teacher and is One who has devoted her life to helping others.

Eugene N. Crone, Ph.D.

ACKNOWLEDGEMENTS

I wish to thank the many family members, colleagues, friends, worship participants and Recovering members of the Deaf Community for their support, contributions, and patience in the Preparation and research of this Book.

Alcoholics Anonymous

National Deaf Academy Administration and Staff

Dr. Carol Goodman, Ed.D.,RTD, C.T.
Professor/Coordinator of the Education of the Deaf
and Hard of Hearing program at Kean University
in Union, New Jersey

National Association of Alcoholism and Drug Abuse Counselors
Mary Woods, President

Dr. Crone presents the book, "They Hear Through Their Eyes"
Co-authors: Dr. Crone and Dr. Carol Goodman to Mary Woods,
President of NAADAC in Washington, D.C.

CONTENTS

PSI PSYCHIATRIC SOLUTIONS, INC.

About PSI   Investors   Facilities   Management Services
Employees   Careers

Visit Our Web Site

National Deaf Academy
19650 U.S. Highway 441
Mt. Dora, FL 32757
352-735-9500 (voice)
352-735-9570 (TTY)

National Deaf Academy
Our Services

National Deaf Academy (NDA) is a residential treatment center for deaf and hard-of-hearing children, adolescents, and adults with a wide range of psychiatric and behavioral problems.

NDA serves an extremely diverse, and at times, neurologically complicated population. The treatment programs are subsequently customized for each resident based on their specific needs, and include treatment for:

- Pervasive Developmental Disorders/Autism (hearing and non-hearing)
- Impulsivity and antisocial behaviors
- Attention-Deficit Disorder
- Post-Traumatic Stress Disorder
- Anxiety disorders
- Mood disorders
- Psychotic disorders
- Developmental delays
- Communication disorders
- Drug and alcohol abuse

In addition to our innovative psychiatric treatment program, the Charter School is uniquely suited to addressing the developmental and language-based needs of this traditionally underserved population. Though a "total communication" model is embraced, American Sign Language (ASL) is the primary language used on campus.

Contact Us
Visit our *Web site* for additional program information, the referral process and job openings.

Phone:
(352) 735-9500 (voice) or (352) 735-9570 (TTY)

Fax:
(352) 735-4939

Address:
19650 U.S. Highway 441
Mt. Dora, Fla. 32757

PURPOSE

This book, "TO RUSSIA WITH HOPE" is designed to learn what Russia is doing for the Suffering alcoholic/addict. Dr. Crone was a member of the team of ten Addiction professionals Selected from across the country to tour treatment centers, clinics, and hospitals in Moscow and St. Petersburg. The first section of this book deals with that tour. In Russia very little is done for The deaf or hard of hearing alcoholic/addict compared to this country. When a Deaf alcoholic or Addict goes into treatment there are few if any Interpreters for the Deaf. Everything is written between Doctor, Staff and Client. Most of the treatment is detox and then they are returned home or a work Program.

In part II specialists in the field of addiction for the deaf contribute to articles on all phases and Modalities of Treatment, and is designed to help and guide the professional, either deaf or hearing, who works with persons who are Deaf to identify the signs and symptoms of substance abuse and help those individuals break through their own denial systems. It is an excellent resource for educational programs preparing professionals to work in the field – including administrators, counselors, doctors, interpreters, mental health aides, nurses, social workers and therapists. Often done in group sessions supplemented by one-on-one counseling sessions, a unique treatment option, "The Support Team," is presented as one model facilitating self-analysis which enhances the client's ability to make that breakthrough. Once the client admits powerlessness over his/her addiction, the life-long process of recovery can be initiated.

Often, Deaf clients will do well in the recovery process while secluded in the protective environment of a treatment facility, but it is not uncommon to deal with numerous relapses shortly before or after discharge. It becomes apparent that the identification of the disease and initial treatment is not enough. Appropriate follow-up services must be provided in the home community. Options for creating effective aftercare plans are provided.

The Vocational Rehabilitation Act of 1975 and the American with Disabilities Act (ADA) address such issues as housing and communication access in public and government services, but they often do not provide communication access in twelve step meetings; it is implied that the community has some responsibility to take care of its own. Alcoholics Anonymous (AA) and other twelve step programs are beginning to accept that responsibility and find avenues for providing qualified interpreters for meetings, as well as sponsors who have worked the steps yet have the necessary ability to communicate effectively with this unique population.

While alcoholics and addicts who can hear have the option of going home to virtually any community in the world and finding "friends" in the recovering community to support their abstinence from their addiction, the client who is Deaf is isolated by the communication barrier of the spoken and written word, as well as the stigma of his/her diagnosis; he or she often returns to the old familiar option – the "using" subgroup of the Deaf community. Therefore, it becomes incumbent upon the treatment team to present appropriate assertiveness skills training and the necessary follow-up services which might include, but not necessarily be limited to:

▶ Housing options in an environment free of substance abuse
▶ Empowering the Deaf client with effective advocacy skills
▶ Locating appropriate twelve step meetings
▶ Establishing effective communication options appropriate for the client

▶ Educating and supporting the local recovery community

The intent is to scrutinize the twelve step process and the twelve steps with implications of how they apply to the Deaf community. Techniques which are an established part of a hearing twelve step recovery program, such as incorporating standardized readings from the Big Book of Alcoholics Anonymous, may have to be adapted for clients whoa re Deaf who may also have limited literacy skills and need a visual format. Alternative suggestions for interpretations are also offered.

Confidentiality, an issue important in all mental health and recovery forums, becomes even more paramount within the Deaf community where gossip travels fast and secrets are difficult to keep. Furthermore, the nature of the Deaf community creates an additional twist for working the steps that the treatment team needs to be aware of.

The format of this text is to first present general information about the Deaf community to sensitize the treatment team to the issues of deafness first, before disclosing the issues related specifically to recovery. It is also a practical guide for professionals, both deaf and hearing, to seek the paths that will provide maximum support for the recovering alcoholic or addict who is deaf, during and after treatment has been offered. In the spirit of AA, the intent of this book is to offer help to the professional community wishing to extend the same opportunity for a life that is joyous and free to those alcoholics who are Deaf. Therefore, this book is dedicated to all the hearing and deaf professionals who attempt to help the client who is Deaf achieve a sober and satisfying life, including administrators, counselors, doctors, interpreters, mental health aides, nurses, social workers, and therapists.

FOREWORD

"To Russia With Hope"
By
Alan M. Cohen, MD
Medical Director
National Deaf Academy

Five years ago, after a professional career that focused on the psychiatric needs of children and adolescents with severe behavioral disorders, a Deaf 17 year old boy (and his interpreter) was referred to my in-patient group for ongoing therapy to address his longstanding difficulties with impulsivity and substance abuse. Feeling airily confident of my skills and the extent of my experience, I thought little of it, and simply assumed the "Billy" would slowly blend into "the mix", and over time, begin to take a look at himself in a more realistic manner than he had previously. Six months later, after "Billy" had thrown a chair through a plate glass window in the middle of a particularly difficult and confrontational session, I was still waiting for the insight and motivation to come-but suddenly, I began wondering to myself what barriers existed that prevented him from progressing as most of his peers had done?

Interestingly, my curiosity regarding "Billy" grew into much, much more, and at the height of my career I gave it all up to actively pursue the psychiatric care of Deaf and Hard of Hearing children, adolescents and adults. Today, as Medical Director and one of the Founders of National Deaf Academy, I have come to appreciate the unique differences that exist between hearing and Deaf individuals – *not* that one group is better or easier, but rather, that because of the fundamental differences that exist in their development and cultural experiences, psychotherapeutic approaches – particularly with Hearing counselors or therapists working with Deaf patients – must be informed by the Deaf perspective, adjusted for language breeches, and generally, be "tweaked" to account for the lack of familiarity that most mental health professionals have for what it means to live in a Deaf world on a daily basis.

"To Russia With Hope" takes readers through both an education in sophisticated approaches to adolescent and adult substance abuse while also educating the reader to the special needs of this unique population. Most importantly, it does so with empathy rather than sympathy, understanding rather than the pity that many of my Deaf and Hard of Hearing patients, friends, and teachers resent so vehemently. Gene Crone has taken his years of experience with all "flavors" of addictions, and has produced a much needed academically oriented work that explains through both example and didactics, how traditional Twelve Step models are appropriately utilized to meet Deaf and Hard of Hearing needs, and he does so from the perspective of openly and honestly exposing his own ignorance along the way, and how he conquered his resistance to appreciating the special aspects of Deaf Culture to arrive at a successful style of intervention.

This is a work that is long overdue, written by what the mental health field typically refers to as the "crusty old twelve steppers". It should be required reading for every psychiatric resident or anyone else that is truly invested in quality care from the perspective of understanding all different levels of patient vulnerability, rather than simply "stuffing" the well known rhetoric down the resistant individual's throat. I applaud his efforts and welcome his curiosity in a field that is long on dogma and short on practical interventions.

FOREWORD

"To Russia With Hope"
by
Maxine Minto, M.D.
Associate Medical Director
National Deaf Academy

The Deaf community has continued to fight an uphill battle to receive the same honor and respect as those who are hearing. A Deaf child reared in a hearing home with no ASL is primed for failure to thrive both academically and socially. The U.S. education system, offers little hope to Deaf students who are being taught in mainstream schools with sub-standard tools of learning. The Deaf are part of a true culture that has existed and continues to excel despite the many obstacles and pitfalls laid in their path.

I began working with the Deaf population three years ago. I have had to learn the hard way that the Deaf are a very proud, yet sensitive people. Many have never experienced an atmosphere of open communication in their native tongue, American Sign Language. As the Associate Medical Director at the National Deaf Academy, I have been honored by the family oriented atmosphere that awaits the staff and patients that enter its midst.

Many of the clients I serve, both young and old have significant substance abuse issues. Many admit to self medicating feelings of depression, anxiety and low self-esteem, as they are faced with numerous rejections, be it from their own families, neighbors and friends. Social rejection, coupled with academic failure, one can only predict that sobriety would be an ever challenging journey.

I have had the pleasure of working alongside Dr. Crone for over eight years. His work with the Deaf has been a exemplary. He meets each individual at their level of understanding and expects the same level of commitment and honesty as he would of those in the hearing world. His AA and NA groups at the NDA are a perfect forum for free expression and a meeting of the minds. Dr. Crone is a formidable asset to both the hearing, the hard of hearing and the deaf communities who struggle with the daily tragedies associated with chronic and debilitating substance abuse.

I tip my hat every day to the man I respectfully call "Gene." He is and always will be the go to guy when you need a helping hand along the rocky road towards sobriety.

Psychologist and Staff Show Exhibit from
Art Therapy at One of the Clinics.

Dr. Crone Across The River From The Kremlin, Moscow

Red Square "Kresneya Plasched" The Red Granite And Black Marble Tomb Of Lenin Located On This Square

*Cathedral Of The Assumption "Uspenski," Located In The
Center Of The Square Of Cathedrals In Moscow, Russia.*

*Grand Palace In St. Petersburg. Catherine The Great
Gave This Palace To Russian Emperor Paul I.*

"A PERSONAL NOTE"

Putting together this second book, "TO RUSSIA WITH HOPE" has been an adventure, therapy, Stimulating and a Spiritual experience. It began with being selected as one of ten Addiction Professionals for NAADAC, (National Association of Alcoholism and Drug Abuse Counselors), From across the United States. The purpose was to visit Clinics and hospitals in Moscow and St. Petersburg, Russia in October, 2005.

After visiting these clinics, hospitals, meeting the Doctor's, Staff, listening to the dedicated Professionals about their procedures and treatment modalities. I thought it would be great to Share this with our treatment teams here in America and I would share with them what we are Doing for the Deaf Alcoholic and Addict here in the United States.

Thus the concepts, ideas and philosophies of some of those working in the Addiction Field was Excited about the project and have made a contribution to this book. Personally, it has been a Journey which has brought me more insight what Russia and our country is attempting to do for the suffering Alcoholic/Addict.

My life has been changed by the teachings of the AA Program of Recovery since September, 1970, including a strong Spiritual based foundation which led me to helping others and working In the field of Addictions and Recovery since 1978.

I feel what was given to me, I am able to share with others.
Eugene N. Crone, Ph.D., MAC, CAP.

PROFESSIONAL INSIGHTS

By Mary R. Woods RNC, LADC, MSHS, NAADAC President
News from NAADAC, The Association for Addiction Professionals
Addiction Professionals' Delegation to Russia

Zdrastvuyte! (Hello!) As a result of my involvement with NAADAC, there have been many wonderful opportunities to grow and learn, and I have met many passionate people who love working in our addiction profession. I feel very blessed and honored to have just returned from Russia where I had an opportunity to lead a delegation of addiction professionals to meet and learn about treatment. This has been the highlight of my service to NAADAC.

The trip was organized by People to People Ambassador Programs, a voluntary effort of private citizens promoting international understanding through direct people-to-people contacts. NAADAC was represented by a diverse and interesting group of people: **Wayne Bland, Carole Collins, Eugene Crone, Patricia Garvin, Bob Kajdan, Shawn Kellerman, Christopher Rose, Dewey Skansberg**, and **Susan Taylor**. I am proud to have been part of this team.

The most striking thing about our fellow Russian addiction professionals is the passion they have for their work and how similar we are in terms of beliefs, values, and treatment modalities. They support participation in Alcoholics Anonymous (AA) and are beginning to see the development of other 12-Step groups. The Russian people are reclaiming their history and coping with major social change, and they are a warm and caring people who are very proud of their heritage.

Professional Insights

News from NAADAC,
The Association for Addiction Professionals

Addiction Professionals'
Delegation to Russia

Zdrastvuyte! (Hello!) As a result of my involvement with NAADAC, there have been many wonderful opportunities to grow and learn, and I have met many passionate people who love working in our addiction profession. I feel very blessed and honored to have just returned from Russia where I had an opportunity to lead a delegation of addiction professionals to meet and learn about treatment. This has been the highlight of my service to NAADAC.

The trip was organized by People to People Ambassador Programs, a voluntary effort of private citizens promoting international understanding through direct people-to-people contacts. NAADAC was represented by a diverse and interesting group of people: **Wayne Bland, Carole Collins, Eugene Crone, Patricia Garvin, Bob Kajdan, Shawn Kellerman, Christopher Rose, Dewey Skansberg**, and **Susan Taylor**. I am proud to have been part of this team.

The most striking thing about our fellow Russian addiction professionals is the passion they have for their work and how similar we are in terms of beliefs, values, and treatment modalities. They support participation in Alcoholics Anonymous (AA) and are beginning to see the development of other 12-Step groups. The Russian people are reclaiming their history and coping with major social change, and they are a warm and caring people who are very proud of their heritage.

The highlights of the trip were our hands-on experiences. In St. Petersburg, the City Committee on Public Health told us of efforts to keep addicts' records and protect patients' anonymity. St. Petersburg has separate centers

By **Mary R. Woods**
RNC, LADC, MSHS,
NAADAC President

to treat adults, teens, and children, and clients are seen by medical doctors, nurses, psychiatrists, social workers, and psychologists. We were also surprised to discover that 40% of Russian 18-year-olds are ineligible for military service because of substance abuse.

In Moscow, we met Dr. Yakov Marshak and toured the Kundala Narcological Clinic. Dr. Marshak expressed a desire for our meeting to be a "link in the chain for future collaboration." We also met Mr. Oleg V. Zykov and toured the Russian Charitable Foundation's program "No to Alcoholism and Drug Addiction."

The People to People organization was first-class and met our every need. We were especially grateful for our national guide, Alla Levitina, who became our mother, escort and friend! We met many great people and were fortunate enough to visit four treatment facilities in Moscow and St. Petersburg. ❏

Left: *NAADAC member Eugene Crone.*
Right: *Dr. Yakov Marshak (l), Chief of Department for the City Alcohol and Drug Abuse Center in Moscow, Russia, and Mary Woods, NAADAC President.*

By Mary R. Woods
RNC, LADC, MSHS,
NAADAC President

The highlights of the trip were our hand-on experiences. In St. Petersburg, the City Committee on Public Health told us of efforts to keep addicts' records and protect patients' anonymity: St. Petersburg has separate centers to treat adults, teens, and children, and clients are seen by medical doctors, nurses, psychiatrists, social workers, and psychologists. We were also surprised to discover that 40% of Russian 18-year-olds are ineligible for military service because of substance abuse.

In Moscow, we met Dr. Yakov Marshak and toured the Kundala Narcological Clinic. Dr. Marshak expressed a desire for our meeting to be a "link in the chain for future collaboration." We also met Mr. Oleg V. Zykov and toured the Russian Charitable Foundation's program "No to Alcoholism and Drug Addiction."

The People to People organization was first-class and met our every need. We were especially grateful for our national guide, Alla Levitina, who became our mother, escort and friend! We met many great people and were fortunate enough to visit four treatment facilities in Moscow and St. Petersburg.

Dr. Crone presents the book "They Hear Through Their Eyes" to Aleg V. Zykov, MD., Ph.D., President of NAN (No to Alcoholism & Drug Addiction), in Moscow, Russia on the tour with Addiction Professionals. Dr. Crone co-authored this book with Dr. Carol Goodman, Ed.D., M.Ed, RID C.T., Professor of Education of Deaf & Hard of Hearing, Kean University, Union, New Jersey.

ITINERARY FOR VISITATION AT CLINICS, HOSPITALS IN MOSCOW AND MEETING RUSSIAN DOCTOR'S STAFF WHO TREAT ALCOHOLICS AND ADDICTS

Moscow

Professional delegates will attend a professional meeting at the **Russian Charity Foundation "NAN" (No to Alcoholism and Drug Addiction.)**

The NAN Foundation is a non-profit organization founded in 1987 with regional offices in Russia, Armenia, France, Sweden and the United States. The NAN Foundation is an associate Member of the Public Relations Department of the United Nations with strong collaboration with UNESCO, UNICEF, UN Drugs Committee and other international entities. In 1998 the NAN Foundation received the European-American Democracy and Civil Society Award.

For many years the NAN Foundation has implemented social schemes aimed at the prevention of drug and alcohol addiction, helping individuals with chemical dependency; assisting children in crises, promoting healthy lifestyles, and forming social policies based on public initiatives.

Professional Overview: Status and delivery of addiction services in Russia

Professional program focusing on:

- Cultural differences regarding treatment styles
- Detoxification in multiple settings
- Opiate addiction
- Fetal Alcohol Syndrome

Moscow

A professional meeting will be with the **"Kundala" Narcological Clinic (also knows as Dr. Yakov Marshak Clinic).**

After an extensive research conducted in 1990-1995, Doctor Yakov Marshak outlined a unique substance abuse treatment method which he called kinesiogene therapy. In 1997 he opened a private clinic with the team of the committed associates. Out of the first 10 patients 8 still live in sobriety.

Patients can choose between inpatient and outpatient facilities. The inpatient clinic can currently take 40 patients. Treatment is strictly confidential and includes a special program for the relatives of the patient.

Clinic rehabilitation program utilizes a comprehensive effect on biological, psychological and social aspects of the illness. It is the analysis of the biological aspects of the illness combined with the individual genetic tests results that determine the specifics of the treatment method. Rehabilitation program starts with the detoxification. Herbs extracts and teas as well as special diet along with the kinesiogene therapy, 12 Steps Program, psychotherapy and after care methods are extensively used. U.S. best practices in this area are also incorporated in the clinic treatment techniques.

Recently conducted performance evaluation research shows that 78.5% of the patients following clinic's recommendations get back to a healthy life style.

People to People Ambassador Programs Delegate Presentation
Mr. Robert A. Kajdam, M.A.C.

Co-occurring Disorders Treatment in Substance Abuse Programs
Professional program focusing on:

- Therapeutic communities
- Co-occurring disorders
- Use of Moderation
- Role of Self-help

ITINERARY OF VISITATION AT CLINICS, HOSPITALS CONTINUE AFTER FLIGHT TO ST. PETERSBURG

St. Petersburg

In St. Petersburg delegates meet with the **St. Petersburg City Committee on Public Health.**

The public health system of St. Petersburg is represented by the municipal and federal medical institutions with various funding sources, such as: budget funding, medical insurance provided by the government or by the employer, citizens' private financial resources.

Over half a million of St. Petersburg citizens use medical or pharmaceutical services daily.

100 hospitals and 400 outpatient and ambulatory clinics, 32 medical research centers, 5 medical universities, 10 medical colleges, 169 state-run and 202 private pharmacies and 7 major pharmaceutical manufacturers are currently operating in the city of St. Petersburg. Over 150,000 medical professionals, including doctors and nurses work in the city public health system.

Professional program focusing on:

- Addiction education and training for counselors and healthcare providers

- Residential Treatment

St. Petersburg

Addiction Professional Delegates meeting was held for the **Saint-Petersburg City Alcohol and Drug Abuse Dispensary No. 1.**

Saint-Petersburg City Alcohol and Drug Abuse Dispensary is a public healthcare institution that provides services on alcoholism and drug addition treatment, clinical examination, and rehabilitation. It specializes in the prevention of alcohol and drug abuse among children and adolescents. The dispensaries also conduct research on finding the most effective drug and alcohol treatment for its patients.

Drug use in St. Petersburg has reached an epidemic level. The process has been involving the younger generation, mainly persons 15 to 18 years old, which in itself increases the behavioral hazard and risk among intravenous drug users (IDUs). Heroin is the most widely spread drug being used mainly through injections. The total number of IDUs amounts to 70 thousand people. The most vulnerable groups of IDUs are only accessed by means of isolation hospitals, clinics and toxicology institutions, as the IDUs are usually taken to the general hospital against their will after come exacerbation of their diseases. HIV-infected IDUs have to suffer double "stigma" and still have no aid, not even the necessary and would-be compulsory after-test consultation. It was proved that the epidemics of drug addiction, hepatitis and HIV-infection are developing in St. Petersburg unhampered and unchecked.

Professional program focusing on:
- Research on addiction
- Evidence-based practices

PART II.

TREATMENT MODALITIES IN THE UNITED STATES FOR THE DEAF AND HARD OF HEARING

CONTRIBUTORS: DR. BILL McCRONE
DR. CAROL GOODMAN
DR. ALAN COHEN
DR. MAXINE MINTO
DR. EUGENE N. CRONE

PREFACE: THE DEAF
CLIENT IN RECOVERY

Common Scenarios

- ▶ A mental health therapist who is hearing works with a Deaf client who h as a co-occurring diagnosis of Borderline Personality Disorder and Alcohol/Drug Addiction. He tells the client to drink in moderation and only smoke one joint of marijuana each evening.
- ▶ A psychiatrist routinely prescribes addictive drugs, such as Oxycotin, to Deaf patients who are professed addicts.
- ▶ A social worker who is Deaf places recovering alcoholics and addicts back into their local communities without regard to the necessary support for maintaining abstinence.

Overview and Application

These are common scenarios which occur everyday, everywhere in all parts of the country and throughout the world. Therapists and counselors who are not experts in the field of addiction – or, more specifically, addiction issues of clients who are Deaf, make treatment decisions which may exacerbate the very problems they are attempting to ameliorate. It is not enough to make a diagnosis of alcohol or drug addiction; the staff working with these clients needs to be educated in dealing with the issues related to the diseases of addiction and the specific needs of the Deaf addict/substance abuser.

In the past, the prognosis was dim for those who had reached the depths of despair in what seemed to be a hopeless state of mind and body. Then, in 1935, the program of Alcoholics Anonymous was initiated on the premise that addiction to alcohol is actually a disease which affects the mental, physical, and emotional facets of one's life. In an era of pharmacology, it is amazing that today millions of people are drug and alcohol free, without medication, as a result of a twelve step program – a program which offers a spiritual solution to a physical and mental malady. However, until recently, no one had seriously examined the limitations or special concerns of using this program with addicts who are Deaf.

Today, approximately 3% of alcoholics achieve sobriety, 1% become "wet brains" or go insane, and the other 96% die of the diseases. Ten percent of the general population is alcoholic with another 20% reported to have problems with alcohol. Those who are addicted to other drugs are not included in this tally. Throughout this text, the emphasis is on terms related to alcoholism merely to enhance readability but in almost all cases the concepts apply to both alcoholics and addicts. Likewise, the twelve steps are presented from the perspective of Alcoholics Anonymous (AA), the first of the twelve step programs. Narcotics Anonymous (NA) (and other twelve step programs) use the same steps but may modify them minimally to accommodate for the various addictions, such as food, people, gambling, working, etc. When necessary, all applicable terms will be used.

DRUG AND ALCOHOL ABUSE PREVENTION WITH DEAF & HARD OF HEARING CHILDREN: A COUNSELOR'S PERSPECTIVE

Dr. Bill McCrone, Professor, Department of Counseling, Certified Addictions Counselor, Dean School of Education & Human Services (1995-2000) Gallaudet University, ASDC Board Member

Reprinted with permission of Dr. McCrone

I must admit that, after many years working with deaf and hearing adult substance abusers, I was taken aback in 1977 by the story of David (name changed), an eleven year old, bright, deaf, African-American foster child. If David's life were a movie, you would not believe it.

David's truancy and troubled home life caused him to be placed in an urban foster home where he lived with five other hearing foster children and an older, hearing foster parent. No one in David's foster home could communicate with him in sign language, his most effective mode of communication.

David was very loosely supervised at the foster home. His truancy continued. He roamed the nearby streets at all times of the day and night. Somehow, David was "befriended" by a hearing neighborhood drug dealer who "protected" the deaf child and learned to communicate with David through very basic gestures. Before long David was using street drugs and being paid by the dealer to be a drug courier. The drug dealer knew that the police would not suspect that a deaf child was a drug courier, and even if the police caught David delivering drugs, the dealer knew the police and courts would be in a quandary about what to do with the deaf foster child carrying drugs. He was right.

I met this boy because the police did catch David, thankfully. The juvenile courts placed him in a mental hospital inpatient program where he was helped in very substantial ways by the deaf Gallaudet University graduate students in counseling I was supervising.

Why was I "taken aback" by David's story back in 1977? Ironically, I thought David's deafness and his communication needs would somehow insulate him and other deaf children from the drug world. Not so. Note that, in this situation, it was the drug dealer who took the initiative to "reasonably accommodate" David's communication needs, not the foster home system.

We work very hard to help deaf adolescents and adults break their slavery to drugs and alcohol. It is an uphill battle. We try to understand why some deaf and hard of hearing youth get involved with drugs. Some are self-medicating for pain relief due to communication frustrations, academic failure, family problems (e.g., the perception that they are the cause of parental divorce), loneliness, anger, pessimism, or abuse. Others long to be accepted, even if it means involvement with peers or siblings using drugs. Still others, the one inappropriately being prescribed Ritalin for "hyperactivity" in low standard schools, may come to think of themselves as sick children who need drugs to "fix" them. Don't get me wrong. A Harvard/Massachusetts General Hospital study (Biederman, Wilens, Mick, Spencer & Faraone, 1999) showed that boys with *accurately* diagnosed attention-deficit hyperactivity disorders (ADHD) who are *appropriately* prescribed Ritalin and other stimulant drugs, are one-third less likely to develop substance abuse problems as are boys with ADHA who receive no treatment.

Now addiction counselors serving deaf and hard of hearing people have teamed up with parents and educators to ask several questions geared to helping deaf and hard of hearing children avoid drug abuse in the first place.

First, are there established risk factors and protective factors in drug and alcohol abuse prevention that families and schools with deaf and hard of hearing children should know about? Second, what are the best generic practices in drug and alcohol abuse prevention with children? How can we adapt those practices for deaf and hard of hearing children? Third, are there special drug abuse prevention initiatives families and schools should be working on with deaf and hard of hearing children? I want to address these issues, and then recommend follow up resources for ASDC parents and grandparents.

Risk and Protective Factors

Do you know that the two strongest predictors of drug and alcohol abuse among children and adolescents are (1) lack of parent-child attachment, and (2) school failure (National Institute of Drug Abuse, 1997)? I take every opportunity I can to remind ASDC parents and grandparents that only about 27% of all deaf and hard of hearing students in the U.S. are leaving school with real high school diplomas (U.S. Department of Education Office of Special Education Programs, 2001). The others receive "certificates of attendance" or they drop out. There is no excuse for this level of school failure in 2003. We will need more than the inadequate federal special education standards to fix the problem (McCrone, 1993). Low standard, low skill, low expectation schools increase the risk of drug and alcohol abuse for deaf and hard of hearing children.

Over 20 years of research indicates that drug and alcohol abuse prevention efforts at home, in school, and in the community must begin with supporting family "protective factors" and reducing family "risk factors."

What is the common denominator in maximizing the "protective factors?" Effective two-way communication with your deaf or hard of hearing child, at home and at school. It turns out that this same research on protective and risk factors applies to youth violence, delinquency, school dropout and risky sexual behaviors, and teen pregnancy.

Protective Factors

Strong and positive family bonds
Parental monitoring of children's activities and friends
Clear rules of conduct that are consistently enforced within the family
Involvement of parents in the lives of their children
Success in school performance
A bond with religious organization
Perceptions of family disapproval of drug-using behaviors in family, work, school, peer and community environments.
Positive child competency experiences such as athletics, school clubs, volunteer effort, hobbiers, scouts.

Risk Factors

Chaotic home environment, particularly where parents abuse drugs or suffer from mental illness
Ineffective parenting, particularly with children with difficult temperaments or conduct disorders
Lack of parents-child attachments and nurturing
Failure in school performance
Poor social coping skills
Affiliation with peers displaying deviant behaviors
Perceptions of family approval of drug-using behaviors in family, work, school, peer and community environments.

Drug and Alcohol Abuse Prevention with Children: Best Practices

It is likely that most readers are familiar with the well-known drug abuse prevention approaches found in schools and the community at large. They work to some degree with many deaf and hard of hearing children if communication is effective. The first approach focuses on "Just Say No" to drugs. For some children, that is enough. For others, "Just Say No" is insufficient. Further, parents and schools must ask the follow up question. What are you encouraging the child to say "Yes" to?

If the message is accessible (e.g., captioned), some deaf and hard of hearing children and adolescents who can ready may be influenced by federally funded school posters and television commercials geared to preventing drug abuse. We have all seen the egg burning in the frying pan message: "This is your brain on drugs." I recently sat in on a remarkable all deaf teen Narcotics Anonymous (NA) meeting where that very message was being debated. More recent, more sophisticated anti-drug public service announcements on television have suggested that even casual drug use supports terrorism. These messages can influence some of the healthier, better informed deaf and hard of hearing children and adolescents to shy away from drugs and alcohol. But in my experience "Just Say No," "Your Brain on Drugs." and "I'm a celebrity former addict doing better now" assembly hall messages have no effect on angry, depressed, anxious, and lonely deaf and hard of hearing youth.

Eight percent of all U.S. school districts and many schools for the deaf have invested enormous resources in D.A.R.E., Drug Abuse Resistance Education. This seventeen-week drug abuse prevention program is delivered by uniformed police officers. The social influence D.A.R.E. curriculum (e.g., resist drug offers) is most often used with 5th and 6th graders. ASDC parents may wish to review D.A.R.E. curricula and materials at www.dare.com D.A.R.E. focuses on understanding the mind altering effects of drugs, the consequences of drug use, changing beliefs about drug abuse, resistance techniques (i.e., ways to say no), building self-esteem, learning assertiveness, managing stress without drugs, reducing violence, combating media influences on drug use and violence, risky behavior decision making, saying "yes" to positive role models, and resisting gang/group violence.

Most school drug abuse prevention programs focus in one way or another on (1) information about drugs and the consequences of using drugs; (2) instruction about techniques for making decisions about drug use; (3) values clarification; (4) managing stress; and (5) alternatives to drugs.

Some researchers, like Its Kreft and Joel Brown (1998) of University of California Berkeley's Center for Educational Research and Development, are skeptical of the long term results of drug prevention programs like D.A.R.E. Brown suggests that teaching children about specific drug categories, physiological effects, and drug cross tolerances may even increase drug abuse among some youth because this information makes them more knowledgeable, confident drug consumers.

If there is even a bit of truth in this criticism, it is one more illustration that there can be paradoxical outcomes to all drug abuse prevention efforts. No one drug abuse prevention strategy is enough. The best drug abuse prevention strategy with deaf and hard of hearing youth is multifaceted and collaborative. All deaf and hard of hearing children should be meaningfully involved with a school drug and alcohol abuse prevention curriculum that uses appropriate intervention strategies at the elementary, middle and high school levels. Meaningful participation includes effective two way and group communication as well as deaf and hard of hearing students asking questions and fully involved in discussions. Meaningful participation includes an assessment of the deaf or hard of hearing child's learning as well as the child's ability to convey what s/he learned to his or her family.

But in my experience "Just Say No," "Your Brain on Drugs," and "I'm a celebrity former addict doing better now" assembly hall messages have no effect or the opposite effect on angry, depressed, anxious, and lonely deaf and hard of hearing youth.

There is More

Given the risk factors for drug abuse mentioned earlier, many deaf and hard of hearing children are at high risk for drug and alcohol abuse. So, in my view, drug and alcohol abuse prevention does not start early enough and is not sufficiently comprehensive in most homes and schools with deaf and hard of hearing students. What do I mean?

The biggest part of an effective drug and alcohol abuse prevention effort with deaf and hard of hearing children starts at home and in the earliest school years and does not even mention drug abuse. Assuming love and effective two-way communication at home, and assuming parents collaborating with high standards schools, drug and alcohol abuse prevention requires helping the deaf and hard of hearing child learn study skills, character education, resilience, optimism, and emotional intelligence. Saying yes to these things makes it easier to say no to drugs later.

Exciting New Strategies

One side of the drug and alcohol abuse prevention strategy coin in working with deaf and hard of hearing children clearly should include meaningful participation in "Just say no," D.A.R.E. and other established approaches. But the other side of the drug and alcohol abuse prevention coin must focus on school success and the skill building strategies that bolster the "protective factors" mentioned earlier.

School Success Strategies

School success efforts require highly skilled, highly ethical, high expectations teachers and school counselors who communicate effectively with deaf and hard of hearing children. They know how to promote learning environments characterized by instructional relevance, meaningful involvement and genuine thinking (Glasser, 1969, 1995, 1998). Effective educators also know that deaf and hard of hearing children need instruction in appropriate assertiveness in asking questions and asking for instructional clarifications in class. The children need study skills and test taking instruction.

Character Education

Given the "risk factor" and "protective factor" research, deaf and hard of hearing children will be less likely to fall victim to drug and alcohol abuse if they benefit from the "character education" (Coles, 1997; Lickona, 1991: Ridely, 1996; Unell & Wyckoff, 1995) that has already begun in Utah, Pennsylvania, New Jersey and New York public schools. Even in a very pluralistic society, parents and schools can team up to promote values that enhance healthy personal development, caring interpersonal relationships, a humane democratic society, and a just, peaceful world. In the classroom we take turns and we don't cheat on exams. We use storytelling about Abe Lincoln to discuss honesty and we read Martin Luther King, Jr.'s "I Have A Dream" speech to learn about heroism and being valued for "the content of our character". Students who volunteer in the community learn altruism. Team sports and team projects teach collaboration and cooperation. The best character education programs teach respect (self, others), responsibility and integrity, cooperation and fairness, peaceful conflict resolution, tolerance, honesty, courage, high expectations, and the celebration of effort.

I recommend Hal Urban's (2003) book, *Life's Greatest Lessons: 20 Things That Matter*, to families that wish to convey particular character education lessons to their deaf and hard of hearing children. Chapter headings include: success is more than making money, live by choice, not by chance, attitude is a choice, goals are dreams with deadlines, there is no substitute for hard work. Read Urban's list, and then work as a communicating family to develop and discuss your own list of "20 things that matter," the values your family holds dear.

Teaching Resilience

Resilience education (Brooks & Goldstein, 2001), is one of the most exciting new dimensions in the fight against drug and alcohol abuse. Simply stated, resilience education provides ten specific strategies that families and schools can use to help deaf and hard of hearing children acquire the ability to cope effectively with stress, bounce back from disappointments, develop realistic goals, solve problems, and relate respectfully with others.

Polio vaccine researcher Jonas Salk, M.D., has said that if he were starting all over as a young scientist, he would still study immunization, but he would study the "psychological immunization" strategies that would help children fight off mental illness and addiction. I suggest that resilience education is one such strategy for deaf and hard of hearing children.

Optimism and "Positive Psychology"

After focusing on psychopathology and mental illness for decades, psychologists like Martin Seligmen (1995) are leading the fight to find ways for psychology to promote emotional health, competence, and optimism. Think of it. Pessimism is a belief or worldview that children can pick up when they begin to think that they cannot win, whether they try or not. Pessimism hardens with each setback and then becomes self-fulfilling. Consider able children born profoundly deaf who give up on school because reading and writing skills seem insurmountable to them. Pessimism hardens further when deaf and hard of hearing children never meet successful deaf and hard of hearing adult role models with whom they can relate.

Seligman offers strategies that promote optimism that include diverse mastery opportunities from infancy on, problem solving practice, rational thinking, and assertiveness training. These skills, when applied at home and at school, are powerful tools in reducing the likelihood of drug and alcohol abuse among deaf and hard of hearing children.

Emotional Intelligence

Another excellent strategy that is easily adapted for deaf and hard of hearing children is Goleman's (1997) "emotional intelligence." Consider this. Goleman's research suggests that I.Q. contributes only about 20% to the factors that determine life success. Deaf and hard of hearing children who can learn "emotional intelligence" skills at home and in school are likely to be far less likely to become slaves to drugs and alcohol. These skills include: awareness of self and others, approval of self and others, managing emotions, mastering responsibility, finding personal meaning, motivating oneself, valuing honesty and ethics, and handling relationships.

Summary

There is no reliable study that shows the incidence of addiction among deaf and hard of hearing people. By addiction I mean a life under the control of alcohol and/or drugs. But it is fair to assume that the incidence of addiction is at least that of the general population, ten to twelve percent. If 1.8% of the general population is deaf and hard of hearing children 3-17, then we have approximately one million deaf and hard of hearing children in the U.S. If the rate of addiction among these children is no greater than that of the general population, we can estimate that about 100,000 deaf and hard of hearing children will become addicted.

This need not be the case if effectively communicating families and schools can collaborate to involve deaf and hard of hearing children in the more comprehensive drug abuse prevention strategies described in this article.

Follow Up Strategies

Parents and grandparents unfamiliar with drugs of abuse can find useful information at http:\\www.health.org/govpubs/rep926.

The National Parent Teacher Association (PTA) has an excellent drug abuse prevention website at http:\\www.pta.org/commonsense.

Need funding for implementing more effective drug abuse prevention strategies with deaf and hard of hearing kids? Ask your school counselor to track down local and state funding resources. For federal and foundation funding lead, to go the web site for the Middle School Drug Prevention & School Safety Coordinators at http:\\www2edc.org/msc/funding.asp.

The National Institute on Drug Abuse (NIDA) has a valuable school-related drug abuse prevention website of http:\\www.nida.nih.gov/GoestoSchool/NIDAg2s.html.

Character education ideas can be found at http:\\www.character.org. as well as at http:\\www.atozteacherstuff.com/themes/character-education.shtml.

Positive psychology resources can be found at http:\\www.psych.upenn.edu/Seligman/pospsy.htm.

REFERENCES AND
RECOMMENDED READING

Biederman, J., Wilens, T., Mick, E., Spencer, T. & Faraone, S.V. (1999). Pharmacotherapy of attention-deficit/hyperactivity disorder reduces risk for substance abuse disorder. *Pediatrics* 104 (2), p. e20.

Brooks, R. & Goldstein, S. (2001). *Raising resilient children*. Chicago: Contemporary Books.

Brown, J.H., Bernard B., & D Emidio-Caston, M. (2001). *Resilience education*. Thousand Oaks, California: Corwin Press.

Coles, R. (1997). *The moral intelligence of children: How to raise a moral child*. New York: Random House.

Doty, G. (2001). *Fostering emotional intelligence in k-8 students: Simple strategies and ready to use activities*. Thousand Oaks, California: Corwin Press.

Gerne, T.A. & Gerne, P.J. (1986). *Substance abuse prevention activities for elementary children*. Paramus, New Jersey: Prentice Hall.

Gerne, P.J., Gerne, T.A., & Gerne-Ciavarella, E. (1991). *Substance abuse prevention activities for secondary students*. Paramus, New Jersey. Prentice Hall.

Glasser, W. (1969). *Schools without Failure*. New York: Harper Collins.

Glasser, W. (1988). *Choice theory in the classroom*. New York: Harper Collins.

Blasser, W. (1998). *The quality school: Managing students without coercion*. New York: Harper Collins.

Goleman, D. (1995). *Emotional Intelligence*. New York: Bantam Books.

Henderson, N., & Milstein, M. (2002). *Resiliency in schools: Making it happen for students and educators*. Thousand Oaks, California: Corwin Press.

Kreft, I.G.G. & Brown, J.H. (1998). *Evaluation review: The zero effects of drug prevention programs: Issues and solutions*. Thousand Oaks, California: Sage Publications.

Krovitz, M.L. (1999). *Fostering resiliency: Expecting all students to use their minds and hearts well*. Thousand Oaks, California: Corwin Press.

Lickona, T. (1991). *Educating for character*. New York: Bantam Books.

McCrone, W.P. (1993). Minimal, vague P.L. 94-142 placement and service standards are increasing the risk of drug abuse among deaf and hard of hearing students. In White, F., McCrone, W.P., Beach, R.L, & Trotter, C.L. [Eds.]. *Drug abuse prevention with deaf and hard of hearing students:* *Volume III*. Washington, D.C.: Gallaudet University Department of Counseling.

Miller, B.G. (1998). *Deaf and sober: Journeys through recovery*. Silver Spring, Maryland: National Association of the Deaf.

National Institute of Drug Abuse (1997). *Preventing drug abuse among children and adolescents: A research-based guide*. Washington, D.C.: National Institutes of Health.

Office of Special Education Programs (2001). *Twenty-third annual report to Congress on the implementation of the Individuals with Disabilities Education Act*. Washington, D.C.: U.S. Department of Education.

Rahrer, J.S. (1999). *Seven sensible strategies for drug-free kids*. Washington, D.C.: Child and Family Press.

Rich, D. (1992). *Megaskills*. Boston: Houghton Mifflin.

Rizzo Toner, P. (1993). *Substance abuse prevention activities*. Paramus, New Jersey: Prentice Hall.

Saarni, C. (1999). *The development of emotional competence*. New York: Guilford Press.

Schilling D. (1996). *50 activities for teaching emotional intelligence: Level 1, grades 1-5 elementary school*. Spring Valley, California: Innerchoice Publications.

Schilling, D. (1999). *50 activities for teaching emotional intelligence: Level 3, grades 9-12 high school*. Spring Valley, California: Innerchoice Publications.

Schuster, S. (1992). *Classroom connections: A sourcebook for teaching stress management and fostering self-esteem.* Spring Valley, California: Innerchoice Publicating.

Seligman, M.E.P. (1995). *The optimistic child: A proven program to safeguard children against depression and build lifelong resilience.* New York: Harper Perennial.

Thomsen, K. (2002). *Building resilient students: Integrating resiliency into what you already know and do.* Sherman Oaks, California: Corwin Press.

Unell, B.C. & Wyckoff, J.L. (1995). *20 teachable virtues: Practical ways to pass on lessons of virtue and character to your children.* New York: Pedigree.

Urban, H. (2003). *Life's greatest lessons: 20 things that matter.* New York: Fireside Publishing.

The author appreciates the constructive feedback from Dr. Norm Tully and Dr. McCay Vernon in preparing this article.

DRINKING AMONG PRETEENS IS ON THE RISE, RESEARCHERS SAY

By Colleen O'Connor – The Denver Post

Nearly 10 percent of fourth-graders across the country have started drinking, according to a recent study.

And, for some, alcohol use triples during the next few years. Just over 16 percent of fifth-graders and more than 29 percent of sixth-graders have taken more than a sip, reports University of Pittsburgh professor John Donovan in "Really Underage Drinkers: Alcohol U se Among Elementary Students."

During the past three decades, another study shows, the average age when adolescents have their first drink dropped alarmingly, from 17.5 in 1965 to 14 in 2003.

"They say they're starting at 8 and 9 years old," said Cheryl Reid, who runs the weekly court-assigned alcohol-education classes in Pueblo, Colorado.

"They say they started hard because they wanted to be part of the group of older kids."

So severe is the problem that the head of the American Medical Association refers to it as "an epidemic" that costs American taxpayers $53 billion each year.

Although the number of underage drinkers has declined slightly in recent y ears, the federal government still considers the number unacceptably high. Last month, officials launched a national awareness campaign to reduce underage drinking, including town-hall meetings in every state.

Although often considered a "rite of passage," underage drinking can lead to risky sexual behavior, impaired brain development, mental and physical problems, traffic fatalities and academic failure.

Alcohol is the most commonly used drug among adolescents nationwide. And a number of different measures suggests teens and younger children now are drinking more excessively.

In his report, Donovan notes a 2002 study that showed 6.3 percent of fourth through sixth-grade students had drank beer, 7.4 percent had wine coolers and 3.1 percent had hard liquor in the past year.

About 70 percent of those who drank each beverage drank it just one to six times in the past year, 19 percent drank it one or two times a month and 11 percent drank it one to seven times a week.

CHAPTER 1

CULTURAL CONSIDERATIONS OF THE D/dEAF POPULATION

Everywhere we find deaf men and women of normal or above-average abilities operating automatic machines, performing simple assembly line operations, or otherwise occupied in unchallenging routines. This stereotype illustrates the discriminatory attitudes of deaf job applicants that are inevitable among slightly informed professionals. (Sussman & Stewart, 1971)

Recovery and Deafness: The Dominant and Alternative Paradigms

Recovery from alcohol and drug addiction entails the acceptance of abilities and limitations, as well as the initiation of cognitive and behavioral changes. For addicts who are deaf, it may imply an acceptance of deafness in addition to the acceptance of the addiction. There are two primary perspectives of deafness: 1) the dominant paradigm which views deafness from a medical model as a loss of hearing which impacts one's ability to function "normally" and 2)

1

the alternative paradigm from a socio-cultural model which views deafness as a cultural and linguistic difference (Kannapel, 1993). As society becomes more culturally diverse and more accepting of the uniqueness of others, this paradigm is slowly shifting toward more balance, but we are still far from achieving a full pendulum shift. Throughout the therapeutic process, it is important not only for the service providers to understand their own perspectives on deafness, but more importantly, it is incumbent upon them to determine which model their clients identify with most predominantly. Table I, A Paradigm Shift, contrasts the two perspectives (adapted from Kannapell, 1993).

Table 1: A Paradigm Shift

(Adapted from Kannapel, 1993)

DOMINANT PARADIGM MEDICAL/ PATHOLOGICAL MODEL	ALTERNATIVE PARADIGM SOCIO-CULTURAL MODEL
Perceived by hearing people and those who identify predominantly with the hearing culture.	Perceived by Deaf people and those who identify predominantly with Deaf culture.
Perception: Disability in need of a cure	Perception: Cultural and linguistic minority in need of acceptance.
Preferred Term: Hearing Impaired	Preferred Term: Deaf and Hard of Hearing.

Label: "deaf" (emphasizes the lack of hearing)	Label: "Deaf" (emphasizes a cultural identity with other members of this population)
Usage: "deafness" or "the deaf"	Usage: "Deaf people" or "People who are deaf"
Communication disorders need to be corrected	Communication differences need which may or may not need accommodating
Language problems predominant	Users of American Sign Language; Members may also be bilingual (ASL and English)

Implications of Deafness: Deaf or deaf?

Ninety to ninety-five percent of all children who are deaf are raised in homes where the parents and siblings are hearing. Not having heard the language used in their homes and communities, these children often have deficient language experiences. (Leutke-Stahlman, 1998 & 1999; Luetke-Stahlman & Luckner, 1991; Paul, 1998; Moores, 1987). "Deaf children growing up in homes where sign is not used predominantly and fluently possess a wealth of visual experience that remains linguistically un-represented" (Livingston, 1997; p. 46). Thus, the linguistic input modeled in the home becomes even more important for the child who is deaf than for the child who is hearing who has the opportunity to "listen to" and assimilate language audibly. Spoken language is not a natural model for the child who cannot hear and does not evolve naturally within the same mental constructs that language does in the visual learner (Easterbrooks & Baker, 2002; Livingston, 1997).

When the term "deaf" is used with a small letter "d", it refers to the audilogical condition of not being able to hear. Generally, people falling within this category will use some form of contrived signed English, including spoken English and speech reading. It may be easy to understand these folks but do not be misled by one's ability to speak with clarity or near normal speech. Because they have been taught to function like "hearing" children, they will often nod as if they understand when they actually might not. When the term "Deaf" with a capital "D" is used, it refers to the community of both deaf and hard of hearing individuals who use American Sign Language (ASL) as their primary mode of communication. Written skills may be limited because English is not their native language, but their mental abilities will often range well within the normal to above average intelligence range.

Linguistic considerations for clients who are considered either deaf or Deaf are especially important and will be addressed in greater detail. What is relevant here is the influence that not having a common communication mode with the family of origin has on the development of those who are deaf and hard of hearing. (Please refer to Appendix A, Glossary of Terms if you need help understanding any of the terms used herein.)

Reflect, if you will, on how much you have learned throughout your life by hearing it through various forms. Children who are deaf have to be taught what sound is and how it manifests itself in both important and insignificant ways. This awareness is often heightened around middle school age; an awareness that is taken for granted by those who can hear without difficulty.

A deaf man frequently told hearing students that he thought something magical was happening in his home as he was growing up. His father would be watching television in one room and suddenly, his mother would appear with a bottle of beer for the kitchen for him. He assumed it was some sort of psychic ability that others had but was not available to him.

In the classroom, a young boy about twelve was amazed to learn that paper makes noise. Each time he attempted to wad it up and throw it toward a little girl across the room while the teacher had her back turned, he would get caught and be told to throw it in the trash. After several episodes, he learned that the teacher did not, after all, have eyes in the back of her head and that paper does, in fact, make noise.

Hearing children often learn about money, expenses, bills, and so forth by not only watching but by listening to their parents talk about budgetary concerns – even fighting over how the family income should be dispensed. When sent to bed, they are still able to hear their parents talking and pick up a wealth of information in that way. The child who is deaf growing up in a hearing home misses these incidental learning experiences.

Consider, too, hot much is gained from the radio. In addition to the popular or favorite tunes one might enjoy, one also gleans information and vocabulary about world events, local news, weather conditions and so forth. Consider what the employees of the World Trade Center must have experienced during the September 11, 2002 terrorists attacks – cut off from all auditory forms of communication, they were left with only the visual chaos their hearing colleagues experienced.

Loss of hearing occurs in varying degrees ranging from normal to profound. The loss has the most significant impact when it falls within the speech range and when it occurs prior to the development of language. Those with slight or mild losses are typically considered "hard of hearing" while those with severe to profound losses generally are typically labeled "deaf" in accordance with the medical/pathological model. The socio-cultural model, however, does not recognize by the amount of loss but more so by how it affects one's ability to function.

The Deaf Community

As a consequence of this unique upbringing (the only member of a family who cannot hear), adults who are deaf often find their place in the world by bonding with others who have had similar experiences. This group tends to identify themselves as members of the Deaf

Community and share, in addition to their similar experiences, a common language, American Sign Language (ASL) and use that language as their preferred mode of communication whenever possible.

There are others, too, who also identify with the Deaf Community even if they have some hearing and are able to speak intelligibly. Because of their training and education, as well as the ability to hear to some degree, they have been taught to function relatively well in a hearing world. However, given the choice, they are more comfortable in the Deaf world where others are more alike, than different, and a common visual language is shared openly.

Children who are deaf who grow up in homes with parents who are also deaf are the natural, or native, members of the Deaf Community. They tend to grow and flourish as normally as anyone does because they share a common communication bond with their family and have other role models who are like them as they grow up. Leaders in the Deaf Community are often those who grew up in deaf homes, providing that they had good parental upbringing, as well. Many of the respected leaders, however, are those who are able to function in both the hearing and deaf world equally well because they serve as excellent advocates when they "speak" the language of the majority and are attuned to the cultural differences that enhance effective interactions.

Deaf culture shared among the members of the Deaf community differs from hearing culture. As mentioned earlier, the awareness, or the lack of awareness of sound, makes a difference in how one functions in the world. Hearing children, for example, are taught not to point and not to talk with their mouths full. Since pointing is a linguistic element of ASL and talking does not require an open mouth, neither of these are taboos in the Deaf community. Furthermore, deaf children and adults are often very noisy because they can't hear themselves. Some of these noises are found offensive to the hearing community.

When deaf adults come into therapy for help with their addictions, they often come with resentments against the many hearing professionals that will be assigned to work with them because of the lack of sensitivity they have experienced by other hearing persons throughout their life. Many a deaf person has been conned into signing a contract for something they had no idea what it was for until they received the bill and went for professional help. The ability to trust, not only as a direct result of their addiction but also their experiences with hearing people who have misled them in the past, may be severely impeded thus having a negative impact on their recovery process.

Hearing and Deaf Clients

Now, referring back to the quote at the beginning of this chapter, we see that many deaf people resort to menial positions in society while others may depend on social security disability to sustain their livelihood. Addicts are often described in recovery circles as "great manipulators, having above average intelligence, and not living up to their full potential." This is often especially true of alcoholics and addicts who are deaf where our hearing society tends to perpetuate their helplessness and restlessness. During the Christmas season one y ear, for example, one perfectly normal deaf couple chose to spend their work income for drugs but still wanted to celebrate the season. They went from store to store "begging" and received, just out of pity, a lovely tree, a holiday meal and all the trimmings, toys for their children, and clothes for the entire family. One especially charismatic Deaf man even convinced an automobile dealership to sell him a late model car for one dollar. (See Schein, 1989, as an excellent resource for issues relating to deafness and the Deaf Community, as well as an overview of the dynamics influencing development.)

Alcoholics and addicts who are deaf are more similar to, than different from, other alcoholics and addicts who are hearing. Each have their own issues that need to be addressed. This text helps to explore some of the unique issues that may be present in the deaf client so that the therapeutic process can be pursued rigorously and effectively.

The Clinician's Perspective

To enhance the therapeutic process, service providers should be, at a minimum, sensitive to the client's own view of him/herself. To assume a person who is deaf uses ASL and has resentments against hearing people is as unrealistic as stereotyping any other cultural minority based on one person you know. Once your own biases and beliefs are determined, then as assessment of the client's own biases and beliefs can be assessed. Glickman and Gulati (2003) present the range of perspectives from rejection at one end of the spectrum to promotion at the other end and support affirmation since it exceeds sensitivity by including "cultural competence, relevant self-awareness, and special knowledge and skills" (cited on p. xi from sue, Arredondo, & McDavis, 1992). "We must respect our clients' opinions and provide them the freedom to seek their own solutions to the problems of deaf identity and politics" (p. xi, Glickman and Gulati, 2003). To proceed with treatment based on unfounded assumptions is to do an injustice to ourselves and our fellow man.

Table 2: Cultural Attitudes toward Clients who are D/deaf

(Adapted from Glickman and Gulati, 2003)

REJECTION	Implies adherence to the dominant medical paradigm; clients may perceive the service provider as an "outsider" not to be trusted

INSENSITIVITY	Ignorance without malice about deafness that often results in the client teaching the service provider how to meet his/her needs rather than focusing on the relevant issues of the therapeutic process
SENSITIVITY	Service providers are aware of some of the basic issues, such as providing basic accommodations and where to go for additional resources without depending solely on the client to explain and educate.
AFFIRMATION	Respectful of each client as an individual with unique needs and developmental characteristics that may or may not be fully recognized at the onset of the therapeutic process
PROMOTION	Promotes only the alternative paradigm but not all clients identify solely with the Deaf Community thereby resulting in a form of disrespect.

While Glickman and Gulati (2003) support cultural affirmation, we also understand that it is not possible to acquire a working knowledge of the spectrum of deafness in a few weeks or even months; that would take years of interaction with members of the Deaf community and a experience with a variety of persons who are deaf and hard of hearing. Therefore, we suggest that clinicians and service providers who find themselves working with clients who are deaf be culturally sensitive to the diverse needs of the individuals and tap into the local resources available to them for assistance in best meeting their clients' needs without putting an undue hardship on the clients themselves. This book is designed to help service providers know what questions to ask and where to find the answers.

About ASL

It is not uncommon for the colleagues and professionals working with a person who is deaf for the first time to become excited and determined to learn sign language to communicate. Administrators will often sponsor sign language classes in hopes of defraying the cost of later using an interpreter. These efforts are good and usually greatly appreciated but their limitations need to be understood.

First, not all people who are deaf use ASL and not all teachers who profess to teach ASL actually know ALS themselves. There are many variations to ASL, including a multitude of signed English forms. Like any language, it takes approximately five to seven years to become fluent in the use of ASL 1(because it is another language) assuming that immersion with the Deaf community, or at least regular interaction with native ASL users, takes place.

Learning the language entails more than just learning the letters of the alphabet and the numbers. It is more than just a word-to-sign correlation. ASL has its own structure and grammar that is unique to itself and quite different than English. Because it is a visually-based language, rather than auditory, unique paralinguistic features are often difficult to learn. Paralinguistic features include such things as the rules for when to raise or lower eyebrows, how to use space to effectively convey important information, and what it means when eye gaze shifts from one location to another. Many adverbs, for example, are not found in words but are actually incorporated as part of the verb form.

ASL is not a written language so ASL users often have difficulty reading and writing English. The elements are in both languages but to date, how those elements relate to one another has not been documented and therefore, is not being taught in schools.

Does this mean that one should not attempt to learn to sign? Not at all. This information is offered to help you establish realistic expectations. Most community courses offering ASL or sign teach some basic communication skills to help bridge the communication gap – but they do not provide adequate training to become an interpreter. Recognize the strengths and limitations of the communication skills offered and use them accordingly. Most deaf people are appreciative of hearing people who try to communicate with them. Remember though, your practice should not be at the expense of their recovery. Communication to befriend another human being is admirable; know your limitations and do not attempt to provide in-depth counseling or interpreting services without the proper training and credentials.

CHAPTER 2

LINGUISTIC PARAMETERS INFLUENCING POTENTIAL THERAPEUTIC OPTIONS

Forbidding sign language turned children not toward spoken English, but AWAY from language. (New York Times Magazine, August 28, 1994)

The Significance of Language Development

This chapter explores how a deaf person's language development impacts his/her ability to function in a therapeutic setting. Understanding language development in a person who is deaf or hard of hearing will help the therapist and other service providers better ascertain how to provide effective treatment.

It would be nice if we could just ask the deaf client a few questions, such as, "Do you use sign language and if so, do you use signed English or ASL?" and "Do you consider yourself 'capitol D' Deaf or 'little d' deaf?" Unfortunately, it is usually not that simple as the clients themselves may not know or understand the differences and give misleading responses to such direct questions. For example, it is not uncommon for a person to identify himself as an ASL user if s/he looks up to and respects members of the Deaf community even though s/he may not actually know ASL. Likewise, a person fluent in ASL may say that s/he uses English in attempt to be more like the hearing people who are asking all the questions. Actually functioning abilities and perceptions often differ from their own perceptions of themselves.

Language Development in Persons who are Deaf

Normal, or typical, language development occurs in pragmatic and social contexts beginning in the home. Children who are profoundly deaf typically do not share the language and culture used in the home since approximately ninety percent are born into hearing families (Easterbrooks & Baker, 2002; Humphrey & Alcorn, 1995). The average deaf adult, because English is not assimilated at an early age, reads at about the fourth grade level (LaSasso & Mobley, 1997) making even reading and writing a difficult and cumbersome task. There are numerous deaf adults who have not developed recognized or sophisticated levels of communication due to the mixed linguistic cultures during the formative years of language development (Christensen & Delgado, 1993), and there are as many variations in language use among deaf addicts as there are accents, dialects and languages among hearing addicts.

Many deaf adults use American Sign Language (ASL), as opposed to signed or spoken English, as their preferred mode of communication since it depends on vision (a strength) and not audition (a weakness). ASL users pose a unique problem to hearing therapists because the language is not comparable to English. ASL users may appear to lack intelligence or social appropriateness because not only is their language different, but so are their social norms. Based on language issues only, this group is the easiest to treat when the linguistic and cultural barrier is bridged because these individuals have developed thought and language and are often able to express themselves effectively through the use of a qualified interpreter. The ability of the client to communicate effectively significantly impacts the therapeutic process.

There is another group of signers who, because of mixed language assimilation throughout the years at home, at school and in social situations, use signed English, or Contact Signing, which is the use of ASL signs and often the paralinguistic features of ASL but presented in English word order (Lucas and Valli, 1992). If their language has been fully developed, this group, too, can be easier to work with from a communication perspective. However, service providers are cautioned to not confuse one's ability to speak with clarity with the ability to understand language.

Many alcoholics and addicts who come into recovery also come in with a lack of any formalized language system and communicate superficially without the ability to read, write, sign ASL or use a form of signed English with any regularity; some may have emigrated from other countries, some may be high school dropouts, and some may have used only a form of home signs and gestures at home. That is, they have used gestures and "home signs" to get by in life in their local area but are not able to communicate outside their circle. Home signs are those gestural systems used by one's family and close associates to communicate basic needs. These systems are limited and have limited transferability to other signs of formalized systems. Although there are people who have a limited ability to communicate, we have seen several clients stay clean and sober for years as a result of therapy and the therapeutic community. It is not clear whether it is the therapy that made an impact or the socialization and caring from the other clients who "watched over" them giving them guidance along the way.

Table 3 presents the four main categories of communication used by persons who are deaf and hard of hearing. These are typical generalization, however, and should not be used to stereotype a client. Understanding the various forms of communications may help the therapist and other service providers to be culturally sensitive to the unique needs of the deaf person who enters treatment.

Table 3: Communication Categories

Communication Mode	Characteristics
ASL	Use and understand ASL regularly; Language is fully developed; Reading skills may be limited; Writing may not reflect true intelligence and ability; Usually, ASL users to not attempt to use their voice; Any ability to speak may mislead therapists to believe they can function adequately in English when, in reality, they may not be able to do so.
Contact Signing	Use and understand a mixture of linguistic and paralinguistic features of ASL when presented in English word order; May present with understandable speech; Reading and writing will probably be understandable but look much like that of a person from another country.
Minimal Language Skilled	No formal language development; Limited speech skills; Minimal reading and writing skills, if any. Best communication is through pictures and iconic representations.

Oral	Non-signers; Range in intelligence; Range in ability to speak; Speaking ability may be misleading; Reading and writing may be a communication option depending on intelligence and education; Able to speech read with various degrees of competency.

Client Profiles

In this section, several clients have been selected to represent each of t he above communication categories. In conjunction with their communication and personality profile, we have disclosed the treatment options used with those clients and reasons why. The names and some specific characteristics have been altered to ensure their anonymity.

Brandon: ASL

Brandon, an alcoholic, first came for treatment initially on an outpatient basis. A tall, slender black male in his late thirties, Brandon used ASL fluently but has a charismatic personality which led others to believe they were communicating effectively in writing. He professed to be an avid lip-reader and wrote responses to the doctors and other staff as needed. He commonly shook his head affirmatively when asked if he could read lips; He did the same whenever asked if he understood something. He had become self-reliant over the years and preferred not to use an interpreter.

It wasn't until Brandon was hospitalized that an interpreter was first used. He had misunderstood the need for the medication he had been given and had chosen not to take it with the frequency prescribed; he almost died. From that point forward, interpreters were used for all treatment sessions, including one-on-one counseling, small and large group sessions, and twelve step meetings. The initial work in therapy was comprised of dealing with Brandon's self-sufficiency to help him understand how using an interpreter actually made him more independent, rather than dependent. He became a great advocate for other deaf clients helping them bridge the gap between the deaf world and a hearing therapeutic community. Although a chronic relapser prior to this latest round of treatment with interpreters, Brandon managed to stay sober until he died several years later.

Cassidy: Contact Signing

Cassidy came for treatment to deal with her mood swings when it was discovered that she also used and abused alcohol and other legal and illegal substances. In her early thirties, Cassidy's true drug of choice was "more". Her ability to use some speech, read lips fairly well and communicate readily in both English and ASL, made her a good candidate for treatment. These skills also made her a good liaison between the treatment team and other deaf clients when skilled communicators were not available. She advocated regularly for interpreters when her moods were "up", she questioned authority regularly, and she took a leadership role in establishing outside twelve-step meetings where deaf people can attend regularly knowing that communication is accessible.

Cassidy's moods still cause her difficulty and she relapses but not with the frequency and severity she did initially. She maintains a life outside the therapeutic community but returns for both in and out patient treatment as needed for "tuning up" and to deal with her other issues. When she attends twelve step meetings and works with her sponsor, she is able to stay clean and sober for longer periods of time than she did when she first came for help.

Michael: High-Functioning, Minimal Language Skills

Michael was referred to treatment by an interpreter in a twelve-step meeting. In his early thirties, Michael is a Native American from the mid-west who grew up using home signs and gestures from his reservation. He married a hearing woman and moved to the east where he found work with her family in the contracting business. Michael drank daily out of frustration and was court ordered to attend AA meetings after a barroom brawl. He continued to attend AA meetings but more importantly was brought into the therapeutic community where he began to learn sign language from others who shared his frustrations. It was evident from his drawings and sketches of plumbing and electrical circuitry that he was intelligent – but lacked a formal way to communicate his ideas. Even at his age, he picked up ASL quickly and got involve din the recovery process whole-heartedly. He maintained his sobriety, taught his family and co-workers some basic signs so further enhance their communications, got his GED with the help of a local agency that provides training for the deaf, and the last we heard, was applying to the local community college to get a formal education.

Jerry: Low-Functioning, Minimal Language Skills

Jerry was brought in for in—patient treatment directly from the hospital where he was treated for multiple injuries sustained from a car accident where he had been hit while riding his bicycle across a bridge drunk. Jerry was a homeless man in his sixties with minimal education and even less of an ability to communicate using any form of sign. Pictures were used with Jerry and while in treatment, he attended sign language classes, although his progress was minimal. He accompanied other clients to all therapy sessions and outside twelve step meetings. He was placed in a half-way house with other deaf clients and roomed with a higher functioning client who served as his "buddy".

Jerry had difficulty adapting to the structured environment of a therapeutic community initially but was given accolades and help from both service providers and clients and soon came to understand that he was in a safe environment. His anger outbursts and frustrations subsided in time and he never drank again. Although sober, Jerry died as a result of another car accident where he was hit crossing a bridge on his bicycle – only this time, he was drinking cola and died with many friends at his side.

John: Oral (Late Deafened Adult)

John is what is considered a "late deafened" adult. This means that John grew up, married, had a family and worked as a hearing person all his life so he had learned to read, write and speak English. He was placed on the hearing ward for inpatient treatment from addiction to alcohol and painkillers. Since he had been hearing all his life, his speech was impeccable. His comprehension was limited however and his resistance to treatment made it near impossible to bridge the communication barrier. Therefore, it wasn't long before he was transferred from the hearing ward to the deaf unit to continue therapy.

John was resentful at being placed on the deaf ward and did not get along with the staff or other clients – even those who could communicate orally with him. Although skilled oral transliterators were brought into work with John in small and large group settings, he frequently crossed his arms, closed his eyes and refused to respond. Consequently, he was eventually ostracized by the other patients and not missed when he failed to get back on the van after an outing to a twelve step meeting. It was hours before he was missed and when found, his whole attitude and demeanor had changed. He laughed about the incident and said he realized how much he was missing by being in such great denial over his deafness. John benefited greatly from the use of oral transliterators in subsequent counseling sessions and twelve step meetings. As part of his therapeutic process, John was also taught how to access community resources to get the assistive listening devices that would help him to function more independently in a manner he could be more comfortable with. By the time he was discharged, he had become accepted and appreciated by his colleagues and staff and offered a great deal of insight to other patients who entered therapy with resistance or in denial. John returned to his family and job and when last contacted, he had maintained his sobriety and was living "happily ever after".

Educational Impact

The primary deficit prevalent in children who are deaf is not the hearing loss itself, but rather the lack of language development. In addition to most children having hearing family members during the years most crucial to language development, deaf children enter school where at least ninety percent, if not all, of the administrators, teachers, adult role models, and peers are hearing. Thus, the child grows up in an environment where not only is the language different than what s/he knows, but s/he also feels different from and less adequate than the others. Thus, the charge of the educational system is viewed as the place where deaf children are supposed to learn academics AND language simultaneously. Legislation has had, and continues to have, a great impact on the effectiveness of the educational system.

The Education of All Handicapped Children's Act (1975) was reauthorized in 1985 as the Individuals with Disabilities Education Act (IDEA) giving all children the right to a free and appropriate education in the least restrictive environment. The reenactment of the IDEA (U.S. Department of Education, 1998) resulted in the closing of several residential schools for the deaf. These schools had typically used ASL or other manual communication modes as their primary mode for the instruction of deaf students. Because they were residential, children interacted with other children who used sign, dorm parents who were deaf, and teachers and administrators (many of whom were deaf). The entire environment promoted both language and academic development, as well as providing a forum where the students could fit in, feel normal and grow socially adept.

Unfortunately, deaf schools were closed as a result of the legislative initiatives and parents demanding that their children live at home. In contrast, few residential schools still exist. The interpretation of the "least restrictive environment" often meant that deaf children had to be place din public schools, thus the need for residential programming was greatly diminished. As residential schools around the country closed, students in those programs were placed in inclusive and mainstreamed settings within their local school districts. This change in placement meant that teachers in the public schools were required to meet the needs of their new students; the new students often possessed communication needs significantly different from the students already being served.

The majority of deaf students in public school programs continue to struggle with linguistic issues; their success continues to be heavily dependent upon the support received in the home. The lack of deaf role models to lead the way, as well as teachers who are qualified and able to teach language concurrent with academic subject matter significantly impacts the child's ability to assimilate in a hearing world. It is rare (but not impossible) for a student who is deaf to become a leader in a public school because s/he is seen as an "outsider" no matter how well s/he appears to assimilate.

This feeling of difference contributes significantly to the feeling of inadequacy. Like many other hearing students, it is not uncommon to find solace in drugs and alcohol during the already difficult period of adolescence. If one cannot compete in a hearing world, the false sense of strength and empowerment found in a bottle or pill or needle initially serves to satisfy that void. The new, revitalized feelings transcend words and language resulting in an "I'm okay" euphoria. It is that altered sense of "okay-ness" that addicts and alcoholics share across all communication boundaries.

Educational Placement Options

There are a variety of options available today for students who are deaf and hard of hearing. Parents make the best choice they can for their child based on the information they receive. Often the discovery that their child is deaf results in one or both parents coming to therapy to deal not only with the child's uniqueness, but also with the problems and stresses put on the marriage and family as a result of the deafness. There is stress from guilt, shame, blame, financial costs, and altered family dynamics. Counselors need to be aware of the two perspectives of deafness (covered in Chapter One) to better guide the parents to determining the placement option best suited for their child and family.

Placement options range from residential placement (the most restrictive) to fulltime mainstreaming with no or minimal support. The older the child is, the easier it is to determine the option that is best suited to meet his/her needs because it can be based heavily on the child's ability to hear and communicate and because the child is better able to express his/her own personal desires. However, it is at the younger age when language is being developed that the choice is critical and causes extreme pressure on the parents to make the decision that will work for them and their child. If the child does not develop language during the formative years, there can be debilitating and everlasting effects.

Table 4 delineates the range of placement options available for students who are deaf and describes some of the advantages and disadvantages those placements have on developing language and self-esteem in students who are deaf and hard of hearing. Understanding how an adult was educated may help the therapist to understand some of the underlying issues that arise when a deaf client enters the therapeutic process.

Table 4: Educational Placement Options and Characteristics

PLACEMENT OPTIONS (most restrictive to least restrictive)	CHARACTERISTICS
Residential Students reside on campus during the week returning home on weekends and breaks.	Socio-Cultural Model ASL and Contact Signing used Character development emphasized through competition and leadership Role models of successful deaf adults probable Language development maximized through visual learning.
Day School: Manual Entire school is comprised of students who are deaf and hard of hard of hearing; Students live at home.	Socio-cultural Model ASL and Contact Signing used and visual learning maximized Role models possible After school activities limited to those who have access Busing may be an issue

Day School: Oral Entire school is comprised of students who are deaf and hard of hearing; Students live at home.	Medical/Pathological Model Speech reading emphasized Role models possible Activities dependent on what's available
Day Programs in Public School Full day classes with ages/grades consistent with that offered to hearing students ("school within a school" concept)	Medical or Socio-Cultural Model Oral or Manual Interaction primarily within deaf program Several certified teachers available as a resource After school activities depend on staff
Self-Contained Class in Public School Typically, one class of deaf students in a public school	Medical or Socio-Cultural Model Oral or Manual One teacher is primary resource for staff, parents, and students Some students may be mainstreamed After school and social activities usually limited

Resource Room with Mainstreaming Students attend some regular education classes (e.g. physical education) and take others in a resource room with a teacher of the deaf (e.g. English)	Medical or Socio-Cultural Model Oral or Manual One teacher of the deaf as resource Some students may participate in activities with hearing students when accessible
Mainstreaming with Pull-Out Services Students are in regular education classes for the day but are removed from the class for special support services (e.g. speech therapy)	Medical/Pathological Oral or Manual If manual, interpreting services may be provided After school and leadership opportunities in competition with hearing so generally limited
Mainstreaming with In-Class Support Students attend regular education classes all day with assistance in class as required by the IEP	Medical Model Oral or Manual Interpreting or transliterating services usually provided Student may be assigned an aid Interaction with hearing students varies upon functioning ability of the student

While there are multiple variations of the above placement options based on the child's IEP, these are the most common scenarios. Typically, deaf students who have limited speech abilities and are mainstreamed are less apt to participate in hearing sports and organizations because they are less adept at doing so when in competition with hearing students. Those in residential and day programs where they are in competition with others like them are more able to take on leadership role and often become future advocates within the deaf community. It is not difficult to see the correlation between self-esteem and language development in students whoa re deaf and hard of hearing compared with those who have opportunities to participate fully without special accommodation. The impact on language is immediately recognized at the younger levels while the impact on personal growth is not recognized until later in the educational process. Both influence how effective treatment can be implemented.

CHAPTER 3

COMMUNICATION ISSUES, CONCERNS AND RECOMMENDATIONS

Deaf adults come into therapy with a wide variety of communication needs; ;it is the therapist's duty to find the resources necessary to meet those needs to help the individual reach his/her true potential to becoming a productive member of society. (Carol Goodman, 2003)

Speech or Language?

The Americans with Disabilities Act (ADA, 1992) states that deaf people have a right to communicate in their preferred mode of communication. Not all deaf people sign, use ASL, speak, or write. There is no one method that will work equally well for all deaf people. This is a critical concern for the professional attempting to provide treatment to the individual who is addicted to drugs or alcohol.

The first fact that needs to be addressed is the correlation between speech and language. Speech is one way to communicate language which is the processing of thought – a way to organize the information found in the world in which we live. There are some deaf people who have good speech but poor language. Likewise, there are other deaf people who have highly developed language but poor speech. This often creates a false illusion to the professional working with deaf clients. They often mistakenly assume that the ability to speak equates with intelligence.

There are several factors that influence the individual's ability to learn language: age of onset, severity of loss, and intelligence, in addition to the familial and educational influences in their lives as discussed in previous chapters. Obviously, pre-lingual deafness (becoming deaf before the child has learned to speak) and a severe loss in the speech range will have a more dire impact on language development than in the child who learned to speak before becoming deaf or the child who has only a slight loss of hearing.

Because language development in a person who cannot hear does not develop in an auditory/oral mode as it does with those whose hearing is in tact, deaf people communicate in ways that are visually and manually based. Manual forms may include sign language but in those who do not sign, gestures and writing might supplement the communication process. The point is that effective communication must be visual in some form readily understandable by the client.

It is often believed that deaf people can read lips, yet only about twenty percent of speech is actually visible on the lips. Typically, hearing people are better lip readers than deaf people because they have the predictability of language – something missing in a person who has never heard language before.

In the treatment setting, then, we see that no two deaf people are equally alike and a communication mode that satisfies one client may or may not satisfy the needs of another. Some clients may sue ASL (which takes approximately five to seven years to achieve fluency, Easterbrooks, 2002), some clients may lip read effectively but lack linguistic concepts to understand common vocabulary and terms, and still others may use some contrived form of signed English, or Contact Signing. It would be unreasonable to assume that a therapist or other professional staff member can meet all the needs of each client. Therefore, it is incumbent on the professional to seek the necessary resources to implement an effective treatment plan.

Certified interpreters can often be helpful in assessing the language needs of the client. The emphasis here is on the term, "certified". There are people who claim to be interpreters because they have the basic ability to communicate using some form of sign language. By employing a professional who has been trained in multiple forms of communication, the therapist has the ability to determine what the needs actually are – ASL, one of many forms of signed English, writing, speaking, lip reading, etc. A good interpreter may also be able to ascertain unique nuances indicative of current drug or alcohol use (the equivalent of slurred speech, for example).

The certified interpreter will be most effective if employed as part of the therapeutic team and used, not for discussion on best treatment strategies, but as the language expert determining when and what communication strategies are most effective. The interpreter is employed as a linguistic and cultural facilitator of communication between the therapist/professional and the client who is deaf, as well as to help empower the deaf client to reach his/her independence. There are several considerations and suggestions to enhance the effectiveness of the treatment process when an interpreter is employed.

Legislative Requirements

Each person shall…be treated with dignity as a human being. (Consumer Bill of Rights)

"Deafness" is categorized legally as a disability and is covered under laws protecting special populations. Individuals who are deaf fall within the purview of a "disability" and are ensured, by law, equitable access to services available to persons without a hearing loss. Equal access for the addict who is deaf generally means access to communication and may mean hiring an interpreter. Table 5 provides a synopsis of the public law, its title and its intent; it illustrates the progression of how law impacts treatment of persons who are deaf and hard of hearing.

Table 5: Summary of Legislation

YEAR	LEGISLATION	IMPACT
1964	Civil Rights Act, Title VII	The beginning of implementation of "All men are created equal..."
1973	Rehabilitation Act, Sec. 504	Intended to enable persons with disabilities to access state and federal services without discrimination
1975	Education of All Handicapped Children's Act	Free and appropriate education to children with disabilities
1990	Individuals with Disabilities Education Act (Reauthorization of EAHCA, 1986)	Renamed the previous Act and strengthened it by adding funding for implementation
1992	Americans with Disabilities Act	Expanded Rehab Act to include private agencies but served to reinforce the initial legislation
1999	Individuals with Disabilities Education Act – Reauthorization	IDEA continues to be reauthorized and funded but still has not received full funding since its inception

Many agencies serving deaf and hard of hearing clients are covered under multiple laws. If the treatment facility accepts any state or federal funding, including Medicare or Medicaid, then it must adhere to the regulations within the Rehabilitation Act and the Americans with Disabilities Act (ADA). If no funding is received but the agency employs more than twenty-five employees, then it must adhere to the guidelines in the ADA.

Making services accessible to persons who are deaf and hard of hearing comes in multiple forms, depending on the needs of the clients. Some clients use hearing guide dogs so their canine companions must be allowed entry into the places they go. For residential clients, access usually includes adding visual smoke detectors, turning on the captions on the televisions, and having a tty available for phone calls. These are not particularly difficult or special accommodations; they are considerations that are afforded all clients in an auditory mode that need minor accommodations for those clients who receive information visually. The biggest expense and most significant accommodation, however, is making communication accessible. Often interpreters will be needed to facilitate the communication process in the therapeutic community and the onus is on the agency to provide the necessary services.

Interpreters and Transliterators

> *The lighting quality is essential for effective communication... the interviewer (a.k.a. hearing professional) and the prospective student (a.k.a. the deaf client) should be seated so that they can see each other without difficulty. The light coming from a window should never be to the back of either (participant), because it can cause a silhouette effect. Adequate lighting also reduces eye fatigue, a condition which could cause miscommunication. (Kemp, 1998, p. 26)*

Interpreting refers to the processing of changing one language into another language, such as ASL to English and English to ASL (Humphries & Padden). The interpreter serves as much to the hearing consumer as it does for the deaf client. It is injustice when an interpreter is used who can convey information from the therapist to the client but is unable to render the information from the deaf client to the therapist. Unlike other second languages that are spoken, interpreters are often able to convey the information from the native language, English, into ASL better than they are able to interpret the second language (ASL) back into language. Thus, it is essential that the interpreters used in the therapeutic process have been certified as competent and able to perform the task at hand.

Transliterating refers to the process of changing one language into another form of the same language (Humphries & Padden), such as spoken English to signed English and signed English to spoken English. Since there are several forms of signed English and Contact Signing used by clients who are deaf, transliterators also are certified to perform their duty. In this text, the term "interpreters" is used to refer to both interpreters and transliterators unless otherwise specified.

Oral transliterators are used, as in the case of John, when the deaf person does not know sign language in any form. Since only 20% of spoken English is visible on the lips, oral transliterators are trained to chose words that are easier to lip-read than the choices used by the speaker, as well as how to use gesture and writing to supplement the intended message. Often they are used for large group meetings where watching several individuals exchange ideas is overly taxing and difficult to follow. They are also used, however, in one-on-one sessions where the hearing person is difficult to speech read because of minimal mouth movements, inexpressiveness in general, or even distracting facial features, such as a mustache and beard.

Certification of Interpreters and Transliterators

At this time, there are two certification boards recognized nationally: The Registry of Interpreters for the Deaf (RID) and the National Association of the Deaf (NAD). The certification process is rigorous and is both costly and timely. Interpreters who attain RID certification and the highest level of NAD certification are usually competent to work in the mental health profession. However, they may chose not to if they have not had sufficient training to perform effectively in this capacity. Table 6 delineates the three levels of certification currently offered by RID and the five levels offered by NAD.

Table 6: Interpreting Certification

TYPE OF CERTIFICATION	QUALIFICATIONS
RID CI: Certificate of Interpretation	Certified to interpret between hearing and deaf individuals who use ASL as their primary mode of communication
RID CT: Certificate of Transliteration	Certified to transliterate between hearing and deaf individuals who use some form of signed English as their primary mode of communication
RID CID: Certificate of Interpreting : Deaf	Earned by individuals who are deaf, these interpreters often serve as intermediaries between deaf individuals who have minimal language skills. They usually interpret to a second interpreter who then transmits the message verbally and then vice versa.

NAD V: Proficient	Highest level of performance
NAD I: Minimal proficiency NAD II NAD III NAD IV	NAD offers a range of certifications so those who have basic interpreting skills can achieve a level. It is important to use only a Level V or a Level IV who has had strong training in the mental health setting.

Code of Ethics for Interpreters

Interpreters are professionals and by achieving certification, they demonstrate a working knowledge of the professional Code of Ethics (see Appendix A, Code of Ethics). Based on our experience, we have delineated the following chart (Table 7) showing what is and is not within the realm of an interpreter's responsibilities. If you or your agency find that you are serving numerous deaf client's, it is recommended that you hire one or more interpreters to work with you on an on-going basis. The use of contract interpreters in comparison with staff interpreters will be discussed.

Table 7: Responsibilities of the Interpreter

RESPONSIBILITIES	DO NOT ASK THE INTERPRETER:
To serve as the communication and cultural bridge between hearing and deaf parties	...to "tell him" or "tell her". The interpreter should sign what you are saying while you speak directly to the client; When the interpreter says, "I", it is the deaf person's words – not the interpreter.

To render the message faithfully with the spirit and intent of all speakers.	...to interject his/her personal opinion on any matters relating to treatment. Remember, everything you say will be conveyed accordingly so be careful about having a private conversation in front of a deaf client.
To serve on behalf of all participants equally.	...to be alone with the client. When you leave the room, ask the interpreter to leave as well. This will alleviate the deaf consumer telling him/her facts that should be conveyed to a treatment professional.
To accept remuneration appropriate to the fees charged by other interpreters for comparable services in the area.	...to volunteer his/her time. They are professionals and should be compensated accordingly.
To accept assignments for which they are trained and qualified.	...to interpret in situations where s/he feels she is not qualified. A second interpreter may be needed.
To interpret for less than two hours for any given assignment without a break.	...to interpret for extended periods of time. More than two hours requires the addition of a second interpreter. Breaks should be given to avoid mental and physical fatigue and illness.

To maintain the confidentiality of all assignment-related information.	...to repeat information which was interpreted in other settings; ask the other professional or the deaf consumer, if necessary.

Staff Interpreters vs. Freelance Interpreters

Interpreters are typically employed as independent contractors and refer to themselves as interpreters in private practice or freelance interpreters. Some interpreters negotiate their own rates independently while others contract directly with an agency. Whether working with an agency or an independent contractor, there are set fees and conditions; special terms and conditions may be negotiated, especially if the contract is for an extended period of time. Usually, there is a two hour minimum charge plus mileage for an interpreter. When the interpreter is to work more than a two hour block of time, a second interpreter may be required. There are usually additional charges for evening or emergency calls. Cancellations made within twenty-four hours of the assignment are usually billed since the interpreter's time has been scheduled and another job to fill the assigned time slot might be difficult to obtain. Fees for interpreting services vary widely depending on the agency, interpreter's qualifications (in some cases), amount of time contracted, and area of the country.

Freelance interpreters tend to adhere strictly to the Code of Ethics and will not divulge information shared from one setting to the next, but there may be difficulty in getting clients to open up in front of someone they do not know. If the interpreter is certified and known to be trustworthy, Deaf clients may be more apt to open up and talk sincerely than they will if the interpreter is friendly and conversational. Professional certified interpreters are polite yet have strong boundaries and are not easily drawn into situations which can cause conflict with what transpires and the Code of Ethics.

Staff interpreters, on the other hand, may have different rules and guidelines. First of all, they tend to have a little more leeway than freelance interpreters who are hired on an occasional basis independently or from an agency. As staff, they can be asked to accompany the deaf client to various other support services, such as doctor's appointments, and report back to the therapeutic team on what transpired during those meetings. If this is the case, however, the client should be made fully aware that the interpreter is part of the staff and will report relevant activities observed outside the services rendered during therapy and counseling.

Typically, staff interpreters started with the center as independent contractors and then were later hired as the need for interpreting services was validated. When the cost of hiring freelance interpreters becomes excessive, it may become cost-effective to hire the interpreter on a contract basis, either full or part-time.

Many addicts who are deaf can assimilate into the therapeutic community effectively when a qualified interpreter participates in the recovery process. A professionally trained interpreter can be a great asset to the therapist, client and others in treatment by facilitating communication and handling all the incidentals which can and do affect the treatment process, such as the positioning of clients for maximum benefit to all parties. Not only lighting, as cited in the above quote, but for maximizing participation and equity comparable to that of hearing clients who enter the process. When integrated successfully, communication transpires normally between the therapist, all clients, deaf and hearing, and significant others. The most effective interpreter is one who has been invisible during the interpreted session, yet all the members of the interaction had an equal "voice" (Humphrey and Alcorn, 1995).

Qualified interpreters adhere to an ethical code of conduct which, in part, requires that an interpreter refrain from interpreting in situations when not adequately trained to meet the needs of the assignment. Family members, for example, should not be used as interpreters. A professional interpreter from outside the family allows the client to communicate fluently and deal confidentially with any contributing factors which may arise from unresolved family issues.

If it has been determined that the services of an interpreter are needed and a qualified interpreter has been procured, the clinician and interpreter should meet prior to the initial session to clarify roles and responsibilities. The interpreter is responsible for sharing linguistic information just as the clinician is responsible for the therapeutic process.

CHAPTER 4

SIGNS AND SYMPTOMS OF THE ALCOHOLIC OR ADDICT

I tried to commit myself to a hospital for depression, was sedated and sent home. I was stopped for drunk driving and thrown out of several bars and taverns for bad behavior. I woke up regularly in places that I didn't remember going to, with people I didn't remember meeting...I drank to live and lived to drink. My promises were hollow and a commitment meant nothing. (Eileen K., 1999)

The disease of alcoholism and addiction has no boundaries as it afflicts persons from "Yale to jail" of all nations, creeds, and abilities. Feelings are universal and it is the "dis-ease" that is at the root of this disease. Thus, breaking through the communication barrier is often easier than breaking down the walls and defenses of addiction.

Alcoholism and addiction are diseases that cause the addicted person to deny the facts that are often obvious to others. There is a fine line between "abusive use" and "addictive use" but the first often leads to the latter if not treated successfully.

According to the DSMIII-R, the characteristics include:
Abuse:
1) The use of the substance at least once a month;
2) Social complications;
3) Psychological dependence; and
4) Pathological pattern of use.

Addiction: Includes the first four plus:
5) Tolerance; and
6) Withdrawal symptoms.

It is not unusual for clients to exhibit a cross addiction, where substances with similar effects are substituted to achieve the same addictive desire (e.g. valium has the same effect as alcohol) or dual addiction (co-occurring), where substances have different effects but achieve an altered state of being. The client who presents with dual addiction is typically more difficult to treat primarily because of the extreme differences in withdrawal symptoms.

Self-Assessment

While a substance abuser may know subconsciously that his/her use of alcohol and drugs is not normal, it is often rationalized and justified to a point of conscious denial resulting in an "I'm okay but they're not okay" resolution. For treatment to be successful, the onus is on the client to personally identify the need for help. The old AA adage that "this is a program for those who want it, not those who need it" also holds true for successful results in treatment. Many times, the client's case manager, employer, friends, and family are well of the problem long before the client is and they can be instrumental in guiding the client toward treatment. Keep in mind that rarely will the client find sustained satisfaction in personal relationships, professional endeavors, coping strategies for life's everyday problems, or in treating a co-existing mental illness while the disease of addiction is active and thriving.

Table 8 reveals a composite of the kinds of questions the professional can ask the client who may be an active alcoholic or addict. Clients who are deaf will often respond more realistically if given examples of the types of responses you are looking for. Therefore, examples of what the question is intended to probe are provided for guidance. Keep in mind that the questions are framed from the perspective of the use of alcohol. However, the term "drugs" or a specific drug can easily be substituted or added to each of the questions. Thus, when the term "drinking" is used, you could substitute or add the term, "using."

Table 8: Questions for Self-Assessment

1.	Do you exhibit a different personality when you drink than when you are not drinking? (Examples: Happier when drinking? Angry or easily agitated when not drinking? Less inhibited when drinking?)
2.	Do you think about what and when you will drink? (Examples: Do you plan your weekend around what and where you will drink? Do you obsess on alcohol when you are not drinking? Do you think about when you will be able to drink again when you are not drinking?)
3.	Have you ever felt guilty about your drinking? (Examples: Have you done things while drinking that you would not have done had you been sober? When you have a problem, do you drink to help plan a solution then feel bad because you didn't follow through?
4.	Has your drinking caused any problems in your relationships? (Examples: Do o there complain about when or how much you drink? Have you drank because you were angry or upset with someone? Have you ever lied about how much you drink when asked?)

5.	Do you drink in moderation? (Examples: Do you have a drink everyday? How often do you have more than one drink? When you plan to have only one or two drinks, does it ever become more?)
6.	Do you ever have black outs when drinking? (Examples: Do you sometimes awaken and not remember everything that happened while you were drinking? Do you ever think you are sober then find yourself lost and not realize how you got there?)
7.	Do you drink to deal with your feelings? (Examples: Do you drink when you are alone to cover the loneliness? Do you drink when you are angry? Do you drink when you are happy? Do you drink when you are depressed?)
8.	Do you drink to change the way you feel? (Examples: When angry, do you drink to forget what you are angry about or to plan revenge? When sad, do you drink to feel better? When nervous or anxious about something, do you drink to help you calm down?)
9.	Do you participate in activities where alcohol is not included? (Examples: How many of your friends do not drink? Do you drink more or less than your closest friends? Do you leave a function where alcohol is not served so you can go somewhere else and drink?)
10.	Do you ever lie, cheat or steal? (Examples: Do you sneak extra drinks to feel like you "fit in" better? Have you ever lied about where money is spent because you used it for alcohol? Have you ever taken money from someone to get alcohol? Have you ever stolen something while drinking?)

Signs and Symptoms

Sometimes the alcoholic/addict will still avoid personal disclosure and tell the professional what s/he anticipates the right answers should be. Therefore, the professional should be attuned to other signs and symptoms indicative of substance abuse. When suspected, the professional may want to submit the information to the therapist to use in confronting the alcoholic more appropriately.

Table 9 looks at the typical signs and symptoms of alcohol/drug abuse.

Table 9: Signs and Symptoms of Alcohol/Drug Abuse

1.	Unusual Odors	The substance abuser frequently reeks of alcohol or marijuana residue that may not be evident to the user. In an attempt to cover those odors, s/he may chew gum or use strong breath fresheners. They may carry mouthwash with them and will often drink it, rather than rinse with it.
2.	Abnormal Pupil Dilation/Eye Contact	When high, it may be difficult for the substance abuser to maintain effective eye contact – either a result of guilt or the drug itself. Eyes that are extremely dilated even in well-lit areas are just one indication of substance abuse. If the person is unable to unwilling to maintain eye contact, it may be an indication that drugs or alcohol have recently been consumed.

3.	Unrealistic Self-Esteem	AA refers to the alcoholic as one who is an "egomaniac with an inferiority complex." This description implies that although the person may appear grandiose, it is merely a cover for the insecurities s/he actually feels on the inside.
4.	Changes in Appetite	Typically, weight loss accompanies excessive alcohol or drug use. The user simply finds eating a waste of time and energy and prefers drinking or using to eating. Although they may frequent traditional outings where others are gathering for the primary purpose of eating, active users often will only nibble or even reject their food.
5.	Legal Problems	Alcohol and drug problems often coincide with a multitude of legal problems, both directly and indirectly. A drunk driving charge is one possible symptom of abuse. Rational, normal drinkers who don't have a problem with alcohol don't get DUIs and DWIs – a concept foreign to many substance abusers. Repeated charges are a sure sign of abuse as anyone with the ability to stop drinking will certainly not drive while under the influence. More indirectly, the abuser may have difficulty paying bills and assuming responsibilities that seem normal to other non-abusers often resulting in legal problems.

6.	Moodiness	Irritability and aggressiveness are common characteristics exhibited by a problem drinker or user – especially when s/he can't access the drink or drug when needed. As the user becomes more dependent on his/her drug of choice, s/he often becomes dissatisfied with others and may even become physically aggressive or violent and head toward additional legal problems. S/he may become quite defensive when questioned, not only about his/her drinking or using, but about anything that indicates a lack of responsibility. This attitude often occurs when the person is not actively drinking or using at the moment but is subconsciously obsessing on when and where s/he will be able to "relax" and "just unwind."
7.	Jekyll/Hyde Personality	One of the questions often asked of the potential abuser is if they have a personality shift while drinking or using. This can be misleading to the user who is in denial. Some alcoholics are happier when they drink but extremely irritable when not drinking. The more common case, however, is that as they drink or use, they become more miserable, or angry, or aggressive. Substance abusers often self-medicate in an attempt to control their mood swings – often comprised of depression to some degree.

8.	Financial Problems and Dishonesty	As mentioned earlier, money is pilfered to pay for the ensuing habit and often results in limited funds available for the family's necessities. To gain money, the user may be dishonest and actually lie about where the money has been spent, or deny that s/he has squandered it away on his habit. This dishonesty becomes a habit so strong that it often permeates into other areas, even when telling the truth would result in no consequences.
9.	Employment	Many alcoholics are labeled "functional" because they have not reached the point where they no longer have a job. However, employment problems often exist even with those who still have their jobs. Employers may identify the drinking directly as a cause, or may identify one or more of the other symptoms listed herein as a reason to reprimand the employee. The more noticeable problems are in those who are unable to keep a job, change jobs frequently, or are unable to procure suitable employment.

10	Relationships	The alcoholic/addict often has difficulty sustaining healthy, long-term relationships. When married, the marriage does not have to end in divorce for marital discord to exist. Affairs, indiscretions and other improprieties are common as the spouse and others are often blamed for the abuser's problems. Often the abuser will become either overly submissive, passive, or aggressive in an unconscious attempt to stabilize his behavior and avoid the mood swings.
11.	Self-Sufficiency and Isolation	As the addiction progresses, the abuser tends to isolate more and more. S/he may adopt an attitude of self-sufficiency. "I can quit any time I want. I don't need your help or anyone else's help." After several bouts with the inability to control his/her usage, it may become more evident to the addict how uncontrolled his/her drinking or drugging has become. But that recognition often comes with a price: a lot of resistance and a lot of blame toward others – something family, friends, and colleagues may not be willing to endure.

| 12. | Extremes | There is no peace, serenity or harmony is the addict/alcoholic's environment. S/he tends to react to situations, rather than respond rationally. The further into the disease the person goes, the more extreme his/her behaviors tend to become. S/he becomes more passive or more aggressive; s/he becomes more angry or more happy; s/he becomes more irrational in almost every facet of his/her life. |

An abbreviated form of this list is found in Appendix B: Signs and Symptoms Checklist. As a checklist, it can be used as a quick reference to check which symptoms are present or by adding the dates that various signs were exhibited.

Resources for Interventions

The signs and symptoms, although evident to those without a problem, are extremely difficult to see for the person who is in the midst of his/her addiction. Family, friends and colleagues may help to point them out to the substance abuser and that may lead to the "bottom" necessary to reach out and get help. If caught in time, it could even help the person to see the need for abstinence – but this is the exception rather than the rule. Interventions do not equate to recovery. However, they may lead the alcoholic or addict to begin to recognize the need for help when there is seemingly nowhere else to turn.

Tough love is easy to say and hard to administer. If you suspect that an intervention by family members, friends and colleagues will be needed, please consider contacting a professional for help and guidance. There are resources listed in Appendix C: Resources for Intervention Support for additional information.

CHAPTER 5

IDENTIFYING AND ESTABLISHING TREATMENT OPTIONS

...the actual or potential alcoholic, with hardly an exception, will be absolutely unable to stop drinking on the basis of self-knowledge. This is a point we wish to emphasize and re-emphasize, to smash home upon our alcoholic readers as it has been revealed to us out of bitter experience. (Alcoholics Anonymous, p. 39).

Abstinence or Moderation

It is imperative that the drugs and alcohol be removed as soon as possible and abstinence maintained because it is impossible to deal with the emotional and mental health issues of a client who is still using. Motivating addicts to give up their drug(s) of choice is not easy, and for addicts who are deaf, it becomes even more of a challenge. In the using community, drugs knew no boundaries; one did not need to share a language to buy a bottle or "cop some dope" so linguistic barriers were often irrelevant. In recovery, however, feelings emerge that have to be addressed. Although there are isolated cases of success, most deaf addicts resent being sent to therapy sessions and recovery meetings where they are unable to understand what is being said and unable to share what they are feeling. Resentments added at this early stage of recovery further complicate the effectiveness of treatment. Thus the issue of deafness, and more importantly communication, needs to be addressed as early in the recovery process as possible.

In-Patient Treatment

There are numerous residential treatment options throughout the country and in every state. They are focused on treating addicts and alcoholics who are hearing, however, and may be perceived as limited by the addict or alcoholic who is deaf, just as a person who is addicted to drugs believes that treatment for addiction to alcohol is limiting. There may still be benefits to the placement option but it will require breaking through the denial process and helping the client realize the benefit of the prescribed treatment.

A client who is deaf entering a residential treatment facility where everyone there is hearing is sure to experience extreme feelings of isolation, difference and despair as s/he withdraws from the substance – the greater the communication barrier, the greater the difficulty in reaching this person spiritually and emotionally. An interpreter is certainly helpful to some degree but is no substitute for the daily interactions hearing patients are privy to on an on-going basis. An astute therapeutic team will be sensitive to the signs of isolation and provide opportunities for the client to vent his/her frustrations as needed.

There are a few in-patient programs designed specifically for clients who are deaf and hard of hearing but they are sparse. At the time of this writing, programs have been identified in California, Florida, Minnesota, New Jersey and New York but there may be others. To find the programs and resources to best suit your individual needs, we recommend an internet web search by typing in the key words, "treatment centers deaf" in the search bar. In-patient programs geared specifically for deaf offenders offer many benefits to those who identify with, or want to identify with, the Deaf community – especially in the much needed areas of communication and understanding. Clients who are deaf but identify primarily with the hearing community may be better served in a local program comprised primarily of hearing clients. The issues of communication continue to be a priority for all clients.

In-patient programs are typically three to six weeks in length to give the client an opportunity to abstain from substance abuse while learning about the addiction and learning to deal with many of the feelings that were suppressed while actively abusing drugs or alcohol. For adolescents and addicts with serious other co-occurring illnesses, residential care may be extended for longer periods of time. Continued success outside the residential community, however, is dependent on finding on-going out-patient treatment to help the client re-adjust to life in the real world and adopt appropriate coping mechanisms for the stressed that are sure to arise.

Out-patient Programs

Treatment programs designed for deal clients will also be a useful resource for treating addicts and alcoholics on an out-patient basis. Since contact with others is more controlled, however, treatment in hearing programs can be highly beneficial, as well. If the client is still able to function effectively and just beginning to experience problems from his/her substance abuse, out-patient programs may be able to provide the treatment needed to help the client through the denial process and into the recovery process without the need for in-patient treatment. In such cases, the client typically will continue to use but the attempts to control one's usage become more and more difficult throughout the therapy process. During therapy, issues related to the client's relationships and other problems are addressed but the focus is on helping the client identify his/her dependency on the drug of choice. One strategy for doing this is to challenge the client (who almost will always deny having a problem with drugs or alcohol) to control his usage – subtly requesting longer and longer periods of abstinence. Eventually, the truly addicted client may come to realize that the addiction and correlating manipulations are not worth the effort. Each period of abstinence, no matter how brief, should be acknowledged as a positive step but the challenge for longer periods of abstinence continued.

For the client who comes for out-patient treatment directly from an in-patient program, the client will need help in dealing with everyday life and the triggers that come up that the client automatically associates with using. One client came running into treatment on an unscheduled appointment day in total desperation. She had been riding around on a beautiful sunny day when she turned into a local convenient store to buy a six-pack of beer. Realizing that she had been challenged not to drink, she ran to her therapist confused about what to do since she couldn't drink ever again. Fortunately, a recovery meeting was going-on and the client was invited to join the group. She felt relieved hearing that others had had similar experiences and left sober with the realization that she only had to abstain for this moment and take it one day at a time. The days accumulated into years and today she is a role model for other clients.

The success of out-patient treatment is greatly dependent on the client's willingness to participate, acceptance of the communication modes available, and trust in the therapist providing the treatment.

CHAPTER 6

ADAPTING TRADITIONAL APPROACHES

Tolerance expresses itself in a variety of ways: in kindness and consideration toward the man or woman who is just beginning the march along the spiritual path; in the understanding of those who perhaps have been less fortunate in educational advantages; and in sympathy toward those whose religious ideas may seem to be at great variance with our own...Tolerance furnishes, as a by-product, a greater freedom from the tendency to cling to preconceived ideas and stubbornly adhered-to opinions. In other words, prerequisites to the successful termination of any line of search, whether it be scientific or spiritual. These, then, are a few of the reasons why an attempt to acquire tolerance should be made by each one of us. (Dr. Bob, "On Cultivating Tolerance", AA Archives)

It is important to remember that as professionals in the mental health setting, it is the individual who is being treated – not just the symptoms of a disease. Before we can even begin the recovery process, a degree of respect and trust with and from the individual must be established first. This relationship is greatly dependent upon the ability to communicate effectively. Secondly, abstinence from the alcohol and drugs is essential in order to address the precipitating factors that influence the person's behaviors and issues.

Individual Therapy

Individual therapy typically refers to the one-on-one sessions conducted between the therapist and the client. When working with client's who are deaf, this dyad may include a third party – the interpreter which can change the dynamics of the session.

The client has the right to have an interpreter who can be trusted not to divulge any information from the sessions to others outside the therapeutic community. Sometimes the client will explicitly trust the interpreter to the extent that s/he is unable to distinguish the role of the therapist from the interpreter and may relate information to the interpreter in confidence because they are able to communicate effectively. It is important to try to avoid such disclosures whenever possible but in the event it should happen, the onus is on the interpreter to convey that ancillary information to the therapist at some point. This unnecessary step can often be eliminated by ensuring that the interpreter is never left alone with the client.

The client also has the right to an interpreter who s/he can communicate with effectively. Many times the interpreter will be able to convey general concepts or ideas to the deaf client but is unable to effectively convey the thoughts and expressions of the deaf client back to the therapist. Without accurate input from the client, the effectiveness of the therapist will be greatly impeded. The therapist should attempt to restate what s/he perceives the client to have said, perhaps in different words used by the interpreter, and ask additional probing questions to ensure comprehension – rather than just assuming that what has been voiced by the interpreter. If there are discrepancies or any doubt that the interpretation may not be true to form, a second interpreter should be consulted.

Videotaping sessions, with the permission of the client, may be one way to protect the integrity of the session. When questions of accuracy and communication effectiveness arise, the tape can be re-played and evaluated by a more reliable source at a later date, if needed. This process is comparable to the audio-taping currently conducted by some therapists.

Group Therapy

Group therapy sessions may come in different forms with different needs.

The most common scenario for readers of this text will be the hearing group with a hearing therapist and the addition of one or two deaf clients. When this is the case, the interpreter should sit next to the hearing therapist and sign the discussions in the mode and intent of the spirit that will be understood best by the deaf client. Since the deaf client is outnumbered in this scenario, it is incumbent upon the therapist to recognize the limitations of the communication process.

The deaf client who reads lips can only attend to one person at a time; likewise the interpreter is only able to communicate the expressions of one person at a time. Therefore, turn taking skills are essential. The therapist may ask group members to raise their hands and be acknowledged before speaking; some prefer to use a "ball" or other object that can be easily passed around to indicate who has the floor for discussion.

There is also a time delay for the deaf client to receive the information and then process what is being shared before being able to formulate a response. Therefore, the therapist may want to pause after significant chunks of sharing have occurred and call on specific members for their response. The deaf client should be treated equitably to the others in the group; singling out the deaf client can have devastating effects on the therapeutic process. Therefore, adapting group dynamics should be an ongoing part of how the therapist functions, rather than an exception. These simple procedures and guidelines often prove helpful to the hearing clients, as well, when it becomes the natural way the therapist conducts business. The structure and respect that results contributes significantly the recovery of each of the participants.

Written Assignments

Many therapists employ writing as part of the therapeutic process, especially when adhering to a twelve step program where a personal inventory of past behavior is required. However, some deaf clients may have an aversion to the writing process of past failures in school; an aversion that will create barriers to the desired outcomes. Therefore, alternative considerations may facilitate the process.

Individually, not in a group setting, attempt to ascertain the client's literacy skills. This may be done by conducting simple reading and writing tasks or by asking the client his/her abilities. Be aware that the client may indicate that he/she is able to read and write effectively to "save face." Deaf clients are often aware of the stigma attached to not being able to read and write English effectively so may say they can when they can't. Consider other alternatives, such as making notes for himself/herself only or creating a videotape. The client may feel more comfortable writing if s/he knows that it is for his/her eyes only and will be used as a guideline for discussion in subsequent sessions.

A video camera can be set-up in an isolated area where the client can be encouraged to go and divulge information as s/he is ready. If the room is equipped with a VCR set-up, such as the 13" TV/VCR combination that can be purchased relatively inexpensively at many department stores, will enable the client to review what s/he has taped to reflect like the reader who can re-read what has been written.

When assigning written material to be read by the clients, keep the wording direct. Be aware that complex structures, such as the passive voice, pose difficulty for even the best of readers who are deaf.

The goal is to impart information, not assess or teach reading skills. Keep vocabulary clear and concise. Whenever possible, read the information aloud to the client with the interpreter there to interpret to maximize comprehension and afford the client the opportunity to ask questions.

Integrated Communities

Individual and group therapy sessions follow the same principles for all clients – deaf or hearing. However, the group dynamics may differ significantly in an integrated setting or an all deaf therapeutic community.

One-on-one sessions with a deaf client and hearing counselor may or may not require the presence of an interpreter. In some cases, the client may be comfortable with the counselor, able to speech read and write notes sufficiently, and, most importantly, s/he may prefer to not have an interpreter for those sessions. Others with seemingly better communication skills may prefer working with an interpreter. The preference of the client should be held in highest regard.

When conducting a one-on-one session with an interpreter present, the interpreter should be seated next to the hearing counselor so that the client can look easily from one to the other. The interpreter will not always render the message verbatim to accommodate for language differences, however, s/he should inform you at any time if the message being delivered is somewhat different than what you have actually asked. For example, "Are there any other alcoholics in your family?" can render a variety of responses depending on how it is interpreted since there are multiple ways to interpret the word, "alcoholic". Therefore, the interpreter may need to ask for clarification of the intent of the question so that it can be interpreted appropriately or s/he may advise you of the usage interpreted. However, the interpreter will not and should not interject any personal opinions about the content of the questions or responses given and should be there only to ensure effective communication between the client and the counselor.

The integrated therapy setting is altered somewhat by the inclusion of both deaf and hearing members; the exact dynamic depends on the ratio of the deaf to hearing as well as the personalities of the clients themselves. One deaf person in a room full of hearing people or one hearing person in a room full of deaf people will render virtually the same response: non-responsiveness on the part of the minority group member. If this is the case, the counselor has to be particularly aware of the group dynamics if all parties are going to share equitably in the interaction. In order for communication to flow effectively, it is absolutely essential that only one person speak at a time. An interpreter cannot voice for more than one person at a time nor can s/he sign for more than one person at a time. As holds true for all therapeutic communities, if everyone is talking at the same time, there are no listeners and effective communication is not taking place.

Acceptance

The key to recovery from addiction is the acceptance that one has a problem with alcohol or drugs. However, just as important is ascertaining how the client feels about his/her deafness. Many clients have expressed extreme anger and resentment about being deaf and may be stifled in the recovery process until that essential element is reckoned with. Enabling clients to move through the stages of grief (e.g. Kubler Ross) for having lost what others have seems to help in some cases, although not all deaf individuals have a problem accepting their deafness.

Acceptance of one's upbringing is also an essential part of facilitating wholeness in the client who is deaf. Many times there are resentments against family members for not accepting the client's deafness or for not learning sign language to communicate with the client. Likewise, resentments against the educational system for not preparing him/her to compete in a hearing world are common. These are all issues that need to be probed as part of the therapeutic process. Once acceptance of the client's current state of being is accepted, progressive action can be taken to move forward into the recovery process and begin exploration of realistic goals and outcomes.

Because there are often issues related to the family of origin, the use of family members to facilitate communication is strongly discouraged. In addition to the possibility that they may be part of the problem, they might also not be able to maintain professional distance, appropriate boundaries, and impartiality sufficient to ensure that the client is able to participate in his/her own recovery.

CHAPTER 7

SUPPORTIVE PERSON GROUP PSYCHOTHERAPY

I am not in this world to satisfy your needs nor are you here to satisfy mine – but we need each other! (Carol Goodman, 1970)

An innovative chemical dependency group that helps break through the wall of denial is the "Supportive Person Group Psychotherapy." Support Group Psychotherapy was developed by Dr. Springer from the Psychology Department at the University of Florida for hearing persons which was a new approach to group therapy involving two circles. The inner circle contains staff personnel who function as supportive persons for the patients.

The process is organized in three phases which results in a dynamic process when adhered to in the following progression:

1) a warm-up phase which is consists of a general discussion among the patients and supportive persons;

2) a compression phase to stimulate/support patient interactions; and

3) a decompression phase in which each patient interacts individually with his/her supportive person about group themes.

The sequencing of these functions comprises a therapeutic instrument redefined over a three year period by successive trials. An important feature of the Supportive Person Group Psychotherapy is that it functions as a microcosm for the way in which an active inpatient unit can work as a "school for personal growth."

This process has been revised to accommodate the unique needs of patients who are deaf and hard of hearing and enhance the efficacy of these clients to express their inner conflicts and other emotions. Because many clients have difficulty expressing themselves due to limitations with formal language usage, the supportive person can help them identify and express what they are trying to identify. In addition, many deaf and hard of hearing patients with addictions present resilient levels of psychological denial in the early stages of recovery. Using a single circle to enable the clients to see the signing of each person in the group, it is suggested that four couples participate in the process simultaneously. The supportive person serves as the "alter ego" (speaking for the other person in the dyad) to help his/her partner identify issues of denial, anger, rage, grief, and loss – loss of drugs, alcohol, cigarettes, family members, relationships, and even their hearing.

The facilitator ensures that the group is conducted in clear and simple terms. The facilitator keeps the pace moving; if a client gets off point or lapses into silence, the facilitator moves to another couple. At any point, the facilitator may step in and take charge, ending one couple and beginning with another. No "cross-talk" should be allowed. With larger groups, the facilitator should schedule up to two hours so all participants have time to process adequately. This support group concept was presented at the Southern Counselors of the Deaf Association 2003 sponsored by the National Deaf Academy in March 2003. Table 10 outlines the Support Group process for easy reference.

Dr. Crone was the facilitator for this presentation

Table 10: Support Group Outline

I.	Choose participants, place in couple, and place in circle.
II.	Introduction and explanation by Group Facilitator.
III.	Introduce each other.
IV.	Patients face each other and discuss what issues they want to talk about (i.e. denial, anger, cravings for drugs, co-dependency issues, progress, or negative feelings).
V.	Facilitator asks for volunteers to begin. If no volunteer, pick someone.
VI.	Group I (the supportive person) serves as the "alter ego" making suggestions, encouraging, and supporting the Group II person (deaf or hearing client). Switch roles at different sessions.
VII.	Upon reaching the end of the session, high points or unfinished issues are highlighted.
VIII.	Session ends with each client making a statement about how they feel about themselves. The feeling statement can also be used at the opening of a session so the client can identify how the session may have created a change.

CHAPTER 8

INCORPORATING THE 12-STEP PHILOSOPHY INTO THERAPY

Staying clean and sober –
It's what life's all about…

Staying clean and sober –
Starting a new life…

Staying clean and sober –
Meeting new friends…

Staying clean and sober –
Facing challenging experiences.

Staying clean and sober –
Experiencing new love…

Staying clean and sober…
Isn't it all wonderful???

Staying clean and sober –
Won't you please join us?

Stay clean and sober!

(Gina C., 8/23/96)

Eugene N. Crone, Ph.D., MAC, CAP.

The Disease Concept of Alcoholism

Alcoholics Anonymous adheres to the philosophy that it is a mental obsession for alcohol that compels the alcoholic to drink; once even the smallest amount of alcohol is ingested, however, a physical sensitivity or allergy of the body condemns them to go mad or die if they continue to drink (Tiebout, 1963: 2003). Most people who have a physical allergy to something will work diligently to avoid that substance but not the alcoholic. Alcoholics frequently refer to the altered sense of being they first felt when they ingested their drug of choice. It is that altered sense of being that causes them to obsess on the drug and the desire to return to that altered state by any and all means possible – hence, the mental obsession. The addiction process has been mapped thanks to neuro-imaging procedures now possible. However, the disease affects the whole person – not just his mind. Khantzian (2001) refers to what happens inside the person as "addictive vulnerability." The two physiologic processes are called tolerance and dependence and occur early on in the disease but become much more remarkable as the disease progresses. Tolerance refers to the body's need to have more of the substance to achieve the same effect – that eternal search for euphoria. Dependence, on the other hand, refers to the body's physical discomfort and pain when the substance is not ingested as predicted. Both work together to create the state of vulnerability so that the person, not just the mind, becomes addicted. The disease concept implies that the addiction is progressive and is a combination of nurture and nature.

Khantzian (2001) also points out that each addict finds what drug works best for him/her (the drug of choice), but after a period of time, the desired feeling can no longer be achieved and the addiction manifests itself in more inappropriate and noticeable ways. This "disease atrophy" (as Khantzian calls it) lessens the user's ability of choice as s/he strives to stimulate the nerve centers that are now becoming atrophied. With the more prevalent use of drugs than in the early years of alcoholics anonymous, we are seeing younger people enter treatment. Most street drugs, such as cocaine, interfere with the person's psychological growth and development at a faster rate than regular consumption of alcohol. Thus, the principles applied in Alcoholics Anonymous have been applied to recovery from other addictions, such as cocaine and narcotics. Since the principles (the steps and traditions) are the same for all twelve step programs, only the program of Alcoholics Anonymous is discussed in detail. The applications are universal.

Alcoholics and addicts tend to find a preference for a particular kind of meeting. Although it sometimes relates to the format, there is probably a direct correlation to the people who are in the meetings, their willingness and openness toward deaf people in recovery, and the quality of the interpreter provided at those meetings. However, when questioning deaf clients (ages 14 – 43) about their experiences with twelve step meetings, we received a great deal of individual responses – not unlike those heard from hearing alcoholics and addicts. Some of their response included:

- Traditional AA is outdated as most people coming into AA are using drugs and alcohol.
- AA is a lot more stable with longer sobriety and has developed a value system that is grounded in the disease concept.
- We young people believe AA is for older people; NA is for young people.
- NA was a different language, even a lot of slang, street names, reality experiences.
- I believe I have the disease of addiction. My whole family is addicted. I do not want to be like them."
- I am glad there are different ways to achieve sobriety, not just the AA way.

Alcoholics Anonymous

AA is founded in a three part solution exemplified by its logo: a triangle within a circle. The circle and triangle represents an ancient spiritual symbol meaning "mind, body and spirit together as one." When actions are taken within each of the three realms to harmonize or balance the three, then it is believed that the person then becomes whole.

The three sides of the triangle represent the ways in which a person achieves this balance. One side represents recovery as outlined in the first 164 pages of the *Big Book of Alcoholics Anonymous*; it is intended to address the part of the disease which lives in the mind. Another side of the triangle represents unity which is found in the fellowship of AA and is intended to treat the part of the disease which lies within the body; it is addressed by the set of principles delineated in the twelve traditions. The third side of the triangle is intended to address the part of the disease that resides within the spirit and is addressed through the spiritual concepts called the "steps."

Alcoholism and addiction is a physical and mental malady that, according to AA, is treated with a spiritual solution by the finding of a higher power. The alcoholic has a mental obsession which insists that more alcohol is needed to relieve the discomfort of sobriety. Once the drink is taken, however, a physical dependence is initiated causing the person to want and need more. This dependence on the drink becomes so strong that it takes control over the thinking and actions of the addicted individual and the cycle cannot be broken with sheer willpower alone. Intelligence and knowledge is not sufficient to overcome the overwhelming craving for more alcohol, or in the case of drug addiction, the need for more of the drug.

The alcoholic/addict, in spite of whatever religious belief the client may or may not have at the time s/he enters therapy, has come to depend on his/her own resources for strength and power resulting in a life that has become unmanageable and often destructive to self or others. The premise is that s/he must find a power outside of self while recognizing that s/he is not in control of the events and circumstances that life offers. It is a three-fold process where the individual is required to build a relationship with a higher power, him or herself, and with others in the world s/he resides.

That Higher Power, or the spiritual concept, is the basic premise of AA but it usually introduced cautiously to those who are new to program can adjust to the idea. "God" for example is often introduced as "G.O.D.-Good Orderly Direction" and is used to help the alcoholic tap into his/her goodness and good qualities in an attempt to stop the inappropriate behaviors that have been harmful to him/herself and others. "When I do good, I feel good; when I feel good, I do good."

Interpretations of the Steps and Other AA Jargon

There are numerous interpretations of the steps. One interpretation says, "Trust God, clean house, and help others." Another says that the steps are designed to help a person develop a relationship with a higher power, with him/herself, and with others, in that order. The point is that it is simply not enough to "not drink and go to meetings," although that is certainly an excellent beginning. The steps are designed to help a person look at his or her behaviors and become willing to change them. The recognition of a higher power stronger than oneself is the beginning of that process. (See Appendix F for a list of the twelve steps.)

Many AA's come into the rooms with a preconceived notion of that "God" is or isn't and either believe or not, as the case may be. The program strives to teach each person that s/he has been controlled by a negative spirit – the drink or drug – and that by tapping into a positive spirit that is equally strong, one's life and actions can be changed for the better. The steps help the individual see those powers, or spirits, in ways that are comprehensible only to him/her and become his/her unique recovery experience.

AA's share their "strength, hope and experience" in the hopes that something they say will enable someone who is still in the grips of the disease to identify with them and become willing to look at themselves more openly. Sometimes a person will share a particular event that hits home; other times, the "newcomer" relates to the person's characteristics or personality traits in general. Most of the time, however, the newcomer that begins to experience a profound personality change relates first and foremost to the feelings that are shared. This connection is not usually evident the first time a person attends a meeting which is why you often hear old timer's respond with "Keep coming back!" to all different sorts of complaints filed by a newcomer.

When asked how the program works, AA's will often respond, "HOW." They aren't being smart; they are using an acronym: Honest, Open, and Willing. One has to honestly look at his/her behaviors, be open to hearing how others have changed their lives, and become willing to change their own. AA's do not give advice, however, which is why the term "you" is rarely heard in an AA meeting. AA's speak from experience and provide a strong network of individuals who have recovered in different ways – all beginning with a basic change in behavior. Change the behavior and the mind will, no matter how long it takes, catch up. "One cannot think his way into correct actions, but he can act his way into correct thinking."

Thus, "Don't drink and go to meetings" is frequently heard around "the rooms" (AA meetings). The first three steps are sometimes summarized into "I came. I came to. I came to believe." It takes time for change to happen. The wall of denial is a tough one to break down but can be gradually chiseled away as the user stops using and starts interacting with others in recovery. If nothing else, the person isn't using for the hour or so that s/he is in a meeting and that in and of itself is a beginning worth nothing.

Some of the more hard-core meetings will tell the newcomer to "take the cotton out of their ears and put it in their mouth." This has come about in partial response to treatment programs that have sprung up around the country. The therapeutic approach has infiltrated some AA meetings and some of the old timers don't like it. It isn't about what happens and what has happened to a person – those things are best dealt with in therapy. A twelve step meeting is designed to focus specifically on how to get and stay sober period; it's about action – not thinking. It's about dealing with feelings in an appropriate way without using drugs or alcohol to mask those feelings. It's about creating bonds with other human beings who understand and recognize the desire to drink or use when those strong feelings of discomfort and pain arise. It is the fellowship, compassion and understanding that is shared that enables each alcoholic or addict to "go through the pain" and become a better person because of it. Everything that is experienced can be used to help someone else so "we do not wish to change the past nor shut the door on it." We learn when and where and how to share those experiences so they can help another human being get past their current situation without causing further harm and duress that is caused by substance abuse.

Open and Closed Meetings

Meeting schedules can be obtained by calling the main office or hotline in your area. Many areas have their schedules posted on-line, as well. Phone numbers are also easy to find in the phonebook and on-line. The main numbers are used to provide general information about alcoholism/addiction and meetings can connect hesitant newcomers with regular "old timers." In some cases, AA members will come to a person's home or hospital room to talk about recovery and may even offer rides to meetings. Because of the shame and guilt sometimes associated with having an addiction, there are two kinds of meetings: open and closed.

Open meetings are more for people who want to learn more about alcoholism or addiction. Many times family members and friends will attend an open meeting in hopes of understanding someone else in their life. It is not uncommon for someone attending an open meeting to discover that once they take the focus off the other person, it is actually himself or herself that has the problem. People who attend an open meeting who are not alcoholics/addicts usually do not share nor do they contribute financially to that meeting; they are like spectators and remain as anonymous as the other members. Students learning about recovery programs are frequent visitors to twelve step programs and usually exhibit feelings of insecurity and discomfort – much like the newcomer.

Closed meetings, on the other hand, are a different story. Closed meetings focus specifically on how to stay abstinent and achieve sobriety. Being "dry" (abstinent) and sober (behaviorally changed) are two different states of being; the latter requires "rigorous honesty." There are various stages of recovery, just as there are various stages of the addiction. It is the anonymity of the program that allows the addict to heal without undue shame or remorse from outsiders who do not understand the recovery process. Each person in the meeting appreciates the ability to speak openly and honestly without concern that what is shared will be talked about elsewhere. Thus, the saying, "What you hear here, stays here."

Therapy vs. Recovery

Therapy often focuses on changing one's thinking first, then the behavior, while recovery focuses on changing one's behavior first, then the thinking. It is not difficult to incorporate the two philosophical approaches if therapy supports the abstinence of all drugs and mind-altering chemicals. In one scenario, an addict's recovery process was undermined by a well-meaning doctor. The patient's therapy was consistent with the abstinence model thus supportive of the messages he was given in twelve step meetings. He had been doing relatively well with therapy and meetings until he met with his doctor for medication. He not only was prescribed an addictive pain medication, but the doctor also suggested he used marijuana moderately to help control his pain. This set the patient off into his "addiction" once again and further led him back to his drug of choice – in this case, alcohol. It is not that the use of a drug will always lead to "hard drugs", it is more that the use of one drug will lower the inhibitions just enough to allow the mind to obsess once again on the preferred drug of choice. Once the mental obsession begins, it is difficult to stop it and if just the tiniest bit of the drug is ingested, then the physical allergy takes over and sets in motion the craving for more – the body and the mind both craving that perfect euphoric high.

The primary difference in therapy and recovery, however, is in the process, not the product as both strive for a healthy outcome. Many therapeutic strategies focus on finding the rationale for why a pattern of behavior occurs; recovery, on the other hand, focuses on identifying inappropriate behaviors from the past, mending them wherever possible, and making behavioral changes to avoid repetition. The two can and do blend nicely for many addicts and alcoholics.

In one case, an outpatient who had been attending twelve step meetings regularly was hospitalized after six months of sobriety. The feelings became overwhelming and she became suicidal as she needed to address the issues of sexual abuse from her childhood. She had enough recovery to know that reverting back to drinking and using drugs would not solve anything and chose to reach out for help from a friend and a therapist. She was immediately placed in an in-patient treatment program to focus on the abuse issues. Once she felt strong enough, she began attending recovery meetings in-house, as well. In treatment, she learned that others had similar experiences that she could learn from, and she learned that she can share what happened to her to help others. The shame and embarrassment of the past was confronted, it lost its controlling grip over her, and she "felt free to become the person she always wanted to be." While she doesn't share those issues openly in AA meetings, she is able to share her experience that she needed additional help outside the rooms – a practice the AA strongly encourages.

CHAPTER 9

RELAPSE PREVENTION

If I quit going to meetings, I will drink, and if I drink, I will die. (Donna F., 1999)

I am an alcoholic/addict. I am deaf. I am learning that if I have the disease of addiction, I have to go to any lengths to arrest the disease—the same as if I had diabetes." *(Anonymous, 2002)*

Symptoms Leading to Relapse

Often when treating a mental health illness, the professional analyzes the feelings the patient is experiencing with regard to: negativity, depth, severity, duration, frequency, and intervals between episodes. As feelings re-surface, the client is more prone to relapse because it is his/her conditioned way of dealing with those negative feelings in the past. Occasionally, the extreme highs will cause the same sensations causing the person to want to use in an attempt to prolong the euphoria. An astute professional will look for these signs and help the patient identify them and deal with them as they arise before the relapse occurs. However, alcoholics and addicts, unused to expressing their feelings, may try to hide them and act as if nothing is wrong – because having feelings creates a feeling "wrongness" in the addict.

There is a saying in AA that the first drink will get you drunk (because it starts the physical addiction that causes the cravings for more) and "the first drink occurs in the mind long before it is ever picked up." Therapy sessions and recovery meetings are helpful because the participants in the groups get to know one another and "call each other on their shit cause you can't bull shit a bull-shitter." It sounds harsh but addiction is a harsh reality and sometimes it takes a tough cookie to crack a tough nut. Addicts are known for their ability to con and manipulate situations – whether consciously or unconsciously. Sympathetic family members, counselors, social workers, nurses, doctors and other professionals sometimes fall prey to their lies and manipulations causing more harm than good because the substance abuser can often be so charismatic, likeable, and believable. But the "old timers" who stick to the "basics," as they say, have a knack for staying focused on "abstinence" and "doing the right thing." They recognize the "stinking thinking" that creeps in the addict's mind – the thinking that says it's okay to go into that neighborhood, or sleep with so-and-so, or have just one little drink – all the things that have caused others to fall into relapse with various consequences. Did you ever wonder why alcoholics and addicts keep going to meetings? They keep going so they can remember what the consequences are when someone tried to drink or use in moderation; for a true addict, there is no moderation and it will be proven time and time again.

Relapses come in as many forms as addicts but there are some common traits. First of all, the relapse starts in the mind – with the obsession. People who don't have a problem with drugs or alcohol typically don't spend hours upon hours thinking about when and where they are going to drink or use – they either do or don't but they don't spend hours mentally thinking about it. Those who have been abstinent for a while and going to meetings regularly may feel quite secure with their recovery. One addict enjoyed playing computer games and found his first thought may have come when opening the program for his favorite game. A pop-up advertisement appeared that said, "Is marijuana really so bad for you?" This planted a seed. Knowing how his counselor and the people in AA and NA feel about abstinence, he chose not to mention it to anyone, but it kept rattling the thoughts around in his head: "Is marijuana really such a bad thing? It's not my drug of a choice and it would help me to relax a little." Slowly, he started building resentments thinking that "those people" in AA/NA are "closed minded" and "prejudice" and "not everyone who smokes a little pot is an addict". He began slacking off going to meetings and his need to connect with a higher power become less important. Eventually, h e stopped praying, going to meetings, and sharing in his groups. Sure enough, it wasn't long before he decided he could occasionally smoke a joint and be okay. He knew where he had faltered in the past and sincerely believed he now could control his usage. He began planning how and when he would use. He started off only smoking occasionally but often thought about the next time he would use – planning it carefully to ensure he would not use excessively. Two Fridays later, he decided to join a couple of his old drinking buddies for a beer after work and before he knew what happened, he found himself arrested for leaving the scene of an accident he had caused while driving under the influence of drugs and alcohol.

When no longer spiritually fit, an alcoholic/addict will find it near impossible to refuse the drink or the drug when given the choice. Many will aggressively seek it; others will attempt to control it. Control is a funny thing because it is not so much about the outward control as the mental control. They may, at first, have one or two drinks or one or two hits, and, on the outside, appear to be controlling themselves. (This is the time that non-alcoholics and addicts are especially appreciative.) But the energy expended on mentally planning the next time and rationalizing the next usage is exhausting and will, in the end, take over. Once using, there waits "institutions, insanity and death," unless the cycle is stopped and recovery re-initiated. Unfortunately, not all relapses are recoverable; many die or become incarcerated when they go "back out" (out of recovery and into the addiction). Table 11 outlines some of the signs that may serve as a warning that a person is on the road to a relapse.

Table 11: Signs of Possible Relapse

Isolation	As dissatisfaction and discontent set in, the potential relapse begins to find reasons to stop attending meetings and isolates from his/her peers.
Money	Coming into unexpected money or even a paycheck can sometimes trigger the desire to use.
Irritability/ Agitation	Discontent with recovery. May express thoughts such as, "If this is all there is, I may as well drink/use."
Euphoria/ Pain/ Depression	Users often drink or use because they want to increase or extend the happiness currently being felt ("I'm okay now so I can go back – but this time I'll control it.") or because they want to alleviate the pain or discomfort they are experiencing.
Rationalization	As one prepares to go into relapse, they find numerous reasons for not needing to attend meetings, why it's okay to have "just one" or to explain the need to visit people and places once associated with drinking or using.

Old Behaviors	When a user reverts to some of the old behaviors, such as lying, stealing, cheating, etc., s/he will find it so uncomfortable that a drink or a drug will seem like the only familiar remedy.
Familiarity	Going back to "visit" friends in bars, crack houses, and neighborhoods where the drug was the common bond can trigger the desire to use again.
Benchmarks	30, 60, and 90 days – chips/key tags are awarded because physiological changes are typically experienced at these times.

Aftercare Services

A strong aftercare plan can and does help the client make a successful transition back into his/her home community. For the deaf client, there are some special considerations needed to help smooth out that transition, however, Since the deaf client is often in no shape to do advocacy from a treatment center, a good social worker can lay an excellent foundation and pave the way for integration back into the community. The same considerations for a hearing client apply but with the addition of the necessary resources to make those resources accessible. The extra work needed is well worth the investment.

One client, deaf and blind, used interpreters throughout the recovery process; she had an excellent social worker determined to help her succeed in the real world. The client's aftercare plan consisted of getting set up in an apartment on a bus line, tapping into the local resources for companions/aids to learn bus routes and assist with food shopping, getting assistive listening devices installed in the apartment, setting an appointment with a former employer to get her job back, contacting central office to hire an interpreter for a meeting near her home, and finding drivers from that to pick her up and take her home. In this case, the social worker was deaf and used interpreters to facilitate all face-to-face meetings. The result: the client became independent and self-sufficient, returned to work, attended meetings regularly, made new friends near her home and go ton with her life.

Sometimes, the aftercare plan from treatment to "home" is quite a distance so much of the work is done over the phone prior to discharge. In addition to helping prepare the physical setting for the client, the client also needs to be trained in self-advocacy when needed. The deaf client should be able to make phone calls, pay bills, work, attend meetings and become productive members of society like hearing people do. Most cities have some sort of state or local agency that helps provide advocacy training for deaf individuals and will be available to the treatment facility as needed to educate and provide additional resources.

Using the Phone Network

As alcoholics in recovery re-enter the world, they are encouraged to get a sponsor and several phone numbers of others in recovery. This is for the purpose of being able to have someone to talk to when the urge to drink or use re-surfaces. Using the phone for a person who is deaf is a different matter however because it involves a visual display rather than listening to a voice.

Many deaf adults use a TTY (*tele*t*y*pewriter) to communicate over the phone lines. (Some may refer to this device as a TDD, Telecommunication Device for the Deaf.) This special device has a keyboard and an LED display and sends baud signals over the phone lines. It interfaces with another system like it so anyone else who has a TTY can be called. Even so, its use is limited by the literacy skills or the users themselves.

When the deaf caller wants to contact a hearing person who does not have access to a TTY, they must use what is called the relay service; it is comparable to what telephone operators did years ago. Each state is mandated by law to provide access to a toll-free number for hearing and deaf users to call into to contact another party. The deaf caller calls into the relay center and types the name and number of the person s/he wishes to call. The operator, who has both a TTY and a standard telephone, then dials the number to the hearing person and types the response as it occurs. The operator is a third party used to convey the messages as they are spoken or typed back and forth.

This option is certainly far from optional for all parties concerned but especially the deaf client who is new to recovery and already overwhelmed with feelings of inferiority and insecurity. The addition of an unknown third party further complicates the issue. This is not to imply that this process shouldn't be encouraged, but more to serve as a cautionary point of information and other solutions should be sought, as well.

Most states have a TTY distribution program where clients who are deaf either lease or are given a TTY free or at a very minimal cost. Contact the nearest local or state agency serving persons who are deaf and hard of hearing for more information. To purchase this equipment for your agency, there are several vendors and may be located by doing a web-search of 'telecommunication devices for the deaf.'

On-Line Resources

With the increased distribution of computers, more and more people have access to the internet, to email, and to instant messaging capabilities. This is one option for deaf clients with reasonably high literacy skills but, again, its effectiveness is still dependent on the availability of the person being contacted. Fortunately, AA has established on-line chat rooms and meetings so the deaf alcoholic who is fairly literate can find some help on-line. Unfortunately, there are many deaf alcoholics who are not computer savvy or literate enough to reap the benefits of an on-line discussion. Please refer those clients who can benefit from this resource to http://www.12stepmeetings. com.

Interpreters in Twelve Step Meetings

> *The 12 Step recovery process is firmly entrenched in today's society. The process, literature, and associated terminology at the heart of 12 Step programs, though responsive to change, do not represent dynamic elements to the interpreter in terms of fundamental variation from one assignment to the next. Historically, the interpreter, once experienced and competent in this setting, does not encounter situations that affect this approach. However, there is one variable that could significantly affect the interpreting process for the setting: the expansion of deaf involvement at 12 Step meetings. (Randy Parrish, 1994)*

Although we have talked about interpreters and twelve step meetings already, we must now return to the topic of the two combined together as it creates a different scenario – one that, at the time of this writing, still lacks resolution. There are several problems that arise when a deaf person wants to attend a twelve step meeting:

1) Few meetings are available that have a sign language interpreter provided regularly. Therefore, a search is needed not only for an interpreter but for a meeting willing to accept the interpreter and the deaf person. Adding an interpreter often causes dissention among the hearing group members.

2) Most certified interpreters are not in recovery themselves and therefore are not generally welcomed into closed meetings. Open meetings are of limited value to the alcoholic and addict who is still suffering and in need of great help and a place to openly disclose his/her feelings and concerns.

3) Twelve step meetings are non-profit organizations and may find it cost-prohibitive to pay an interpreter – even those that

are willing to accept an interpreter and the deaf person into their recovery program.

4) "Ninety meetings in ninety days" implies that each newcomer should go to at least one meeting a day for the first three months of sobriety. Finding effective means of communication with such regularity is difficult in even the most populated areas.

5) Certified interpreters qualified to interpret in twelve step meetings and who have the desire to do so are hard to find – even when compensation and acceptance is not an issue.

6) Alcoholics/addicts who are deaf have the same recovery ratio as those who are hearing – they don't all make it. So interpreters are procured and paid whether or not the deaf consumers show up or not.

We do not have solutions to all the problems but we do offer some suggestions that may make it a little easier to establish meetings for persons who are Deaf and hard of hearing.

1) Teach the deaf person to be an advocate for his/her own sobriety. Like anything else, the more investment one has in his/her own recovery process, the better chance there is of staying sober. What you give me is never quite as valuable as what I earn myself.

2) Encourage local meetings and clubhouses to take up special collections for the purpose of paying an interpreter regularly.

3) Find interpreters who are qualified and willing to provide interpreting for meetings in the area. Offer to compensate the interpreter in cash immediately following each meeting interpreted or to allow the interpreter to submit a bill after X number of meetings if preferred. Some interprets will only interpret in non-smoking meetings; some prefer days, not evenings and so forth.

4) If the person is Deaf, suggest that s/he offer to teach sign language to some of the group members in exchange for a sponsor willing to work through the steps. Keep in mind that an interpreter will often be needed for step work.

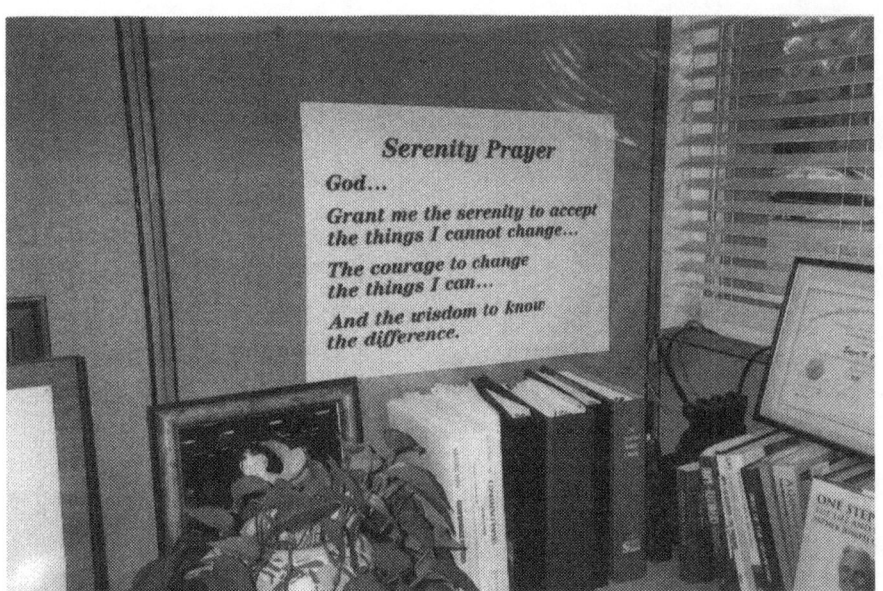

Three For The Interpreter

CHAPTER 10

MELDING INTO THE THERAPEUTIC COMMUNITY

The sign language interpreter should be prepared to deal with very sensitive and personal material in a mental health setting...This will often include issues that are controversial, or come into direct conflict with the interpreter's own belief system. (James Tresh, 1998)

The professional in the mental health setting is an integral part of the therapeutic process and therefore warrants some additional guidelines that will be covered in this section. This chapter focuses specifically on the application of the Code of Ethics in this setting with emphasis on the role and responsibilities of the interpreter and privileged communications.

Role and Responsibilities of the Interpreter

Ideally, all interpreters working in mental health settings would hold the highest interpreting credentials but the ideal is often not realistic. This section is designed to help the uncertified interpreter recognize his/her roles and responsibilities specifically to the mental health setting to avoid creating more harm than good when rendering services. Appendix E provides the Code of Ethics for the profession of interpreting.

1) Confidentiality: It is important that interpreters in mental health settings and twelve step meetings keep the fact that they are even interpreting in such settings to themselves – especially in rural areas where everybody knows everybody and in other areas where the deaf community is close. By just stating that you are interpreting a twelve step meeting, rumors may start up based on pure speculation. To gain the trust of the deaf consumers, it is important that they know you will not divulge any information they have shared – which may include some very disturbing information. Keep in mind you are not the professional in charge and are responsible for the conveyance of the information – not the outcome. To lose this trust could cause the death of the alcoholic/addict who is in need of care.

2) Render the Message Faithfully – Interpreters must remember that they always have two or more clients – at least one of whom is hearing and at least one of whom is deaf. Therefore, information is to be communicated in the spirit and intent that it is rendered by the deaf party to the hearing party and by the hearing party to the deaf party. Foul language directed from the client to toward an AA group member in the middle of a meeting is not to be edited or toned down no matter how inappropriate it may seem. An abrasive, inattentive professional is not to be presented as a kind, friendly person no matter how rude s/he may be. The interaction is to be facilitated as naturally as possible conveying the attitude and personalities of the parties involved – not the interpreter's. If the interpreter is not able or is unwilling to speak/sign in the tone and spirit of the speaker/signer, then s/he should remove himself/herself from the situation and another interpreter contacted.

3) Do not counsel, advise or interject personal opinion. Many times, the interpreter may feel that s/he knows better than the hearing professionals and therefore wants to assume the role of maternal/paternal advisor for the deaf client. Our advice to you – DON'T! The interpreter may, where the deaf client is unable to do so, provide information about advocacy services available to the professional and the client. The goal is to facilitate their communication process and connect them with additional services that may help them in their process. Aside from that, if you, as the interpreter, want to interject your personal opinion about how to get sober, go get a degree! In the meantime, remain impartial and convey the information between all parties in the spirit and intent it was given.

It is important t note here that family members should not be used as interpreters – even when every one gives their consent. Often a part of the therapeutic process deals with family dynamics and the patient who is deaf often has much to say about his/her upbringing – especially in a hearing family. Even if the client felt comfortable expressing his/her true feelings about all matters, it puts the family member who is interpreting in a precarious situation. They may, unintentionally of course, skew the interpretation to appear more favorable than it really is. Furthermore, family members often do not know the language as well as they might like to think – when compounded with mental health jargon, the task can become even more challenging. It is best for family members to be family members and just that.

4) Accept assignments appropriately. Sometimes, mental health jargon is unfamiliar to the interpreter so there is a tendency to, perhaps, spell everything, sign it in straight English, explain it, or ignore it. If this is the case, every attempt should be made to find another interpreter who is qualified to do the interpreting; establishing a mentoring relationship with that interpreter would be ideal. However, if it is not possible, perhaps a relationship with the therapist may be possible wherein the therapist can offer some clarification before

each session. Whenever clarification is needed during the interpretation process, it is important that you state it is you, the interpreter, needing the clarification and not the deaf consumer. Unfortunately, this is often embarrassing to the deaf client and may cause dissension. The same holds true for voicing for a deaf client. Do not assume the message is understood when it is not and do not make up thoughts and concepts that aren't there. Sometimes, a client's language does not make sense and for the therapeutic process to be effective, it is important for the professional to know how the client is processing the information. If you do not know ASL or minimal language skills and the client uses one of those forms of communication, for example, stop the process. If there is any doubt as to the effectiveness of your communication, suggest that the sessions be video-recorded and reviewed subsequently with a certified interpreter. If you do not have enough confidence in your interpretation for it to e reviewed by another professional, perhaps you should reconsider your ability to perform successfully in that situation.

5) Professional interpreters do not volunteer their services; when volunteers are used, it gives the impression that "anyone" can interpret. ASL is a language, signed English is a communication mode comprised of various forms of ASL, on a continuum of various modes of Communication. Professional interpreters know how to ascertain the client's mode of communication and communicate his/her style effectively to the professional. They also are trained in professional terminology and can interpret the professional's language effectively into the language most readily understood by the deaf consumer. They are trained to bridge cultural gaps appropriately, in addition to facilitating the communication process. They are, in essence, professionals that should not be belittled by intuiting that anyone who has taken a sign language class can provide interpreting services. Since it takes five to seven years to acquire proficiency in ASL (Easterbrooks, 2002) and at

least two years of training to be an interpreter, it is best not to undermine the situation by volunteering services. There are, however, some exceptions.

When you are certified and competent to provide interpreting services, you might be wise to offer your services initially at no cost or a greatly reduced fee while you help to advocate for strategies to procure payment or just to show how effective interpreting can be. Once a professional sees how smooth the interpreting process is with a competent interpreter, we are sure your services will be valued and compensation forthcoming. Sometimes, in the case of twelve step meetings for example, it takes a while for the group to understand the need for an interpreter and take appropriate action – which often includes collecting separate donations to hire the interpreter.

6) Function appropriately to the situation. This includes both professional attire and behavior. In mental health, it is suggested that the interpreter match the demeanor and affect of the professional/s in the situation. Furthermore, it is suggested that the interpreter not be left alone with the deaf client – especially during the in-take process or early recovery. When a new client comes into recovery, s/he may not understand the role of the interpreter and just be relieved to have someone to talk to who understands their communication. Hence, they may start to "dump" all kinds of information that really needs to be shared with a counselor or other trained professional. By letting them dump on you, the interpreter, they often find they don't need to share any more with those "hearing" people and will put their trust in you. When you share that information with the professional, you are then viewed as distrustful because what they shared with you was shared in confidence. So your name gets ruined and the client becomes even more damaged than when s/he first entered the program.

7) Professional interpreters continue to grow and learn – just like other professionals do. If you are not one who aspires to improve your skills and become more knowledgeable about

current trends and best practices, then perhaps you are not a professional interpreter and should not be offering your services as such.

8) The goal for any professional is to be recognized by the national accrediting body; for interpreters, the national bodies are the Registry of Interpreters for the Deaf and National Association of the Deaf. Please strive to achieve the national recognition you deserve – and the peace of mind it offers your clients.

Privileged Communications

In mental health, privileged communications generally refers to the "legal procedures for the involuntary treatment of mentally ill persons" (Knapp & VandeCreek, p. 92). However, the concept applies to all patients with the intent of protecting their inherit rights. The patient is given a copy of the "Patient's Bill of Rights" when s/he enters a mental health facility for treatment. The interpreter should familiarize him/herself with these rights and be prepared to interpret them for the client. Generally, the client is given these rights during the intake evaluation and told to read them then ask if they have any questions. To avoid embarrassment, it is suggested that the interpreter offer to interpret them for the client. Ideally, the intake counselor will read each of them allowing the interpreter to interpret from the spoken words. However, this may not be the case so the interpreter should offer to read them herself and then interpret the meaning and intent to the client. A sample of these rights is provided in Appendix D: Consumer Bill of Rights. The exact copy used by the program can be obtained by contacting the person or office responsible for conducting intake interviews with potential clients.

CHAPTER 11

INTERPRETING FROZEN TEXT

God grant me the serenity to accept the things I cannot change, the courage to change the things I can, and the wisdom to know the difference. (The short version of the Serenity Prayer often recited in AA meetings).

There are numerous pieces of literature and sayings that are recited during AA and NA meetings. Interpreters new to mental health settings often ask for interpretations for these excerpts. Information that never changes is referred to as "frozen text". While the text doesn't change, the interpretation could possibly change depending on the mode of communication used by the deaf client. Once the client understands the basic meaning and intent of the text message, a standard interpretation can be used once again. Unfortunately, glossing is not an exact science so even glossing possible interpretations can leave much to the imagination. Nevertheless, Appendix F and Appendix G offer possible interpretations for the 12 Steps and 12 Traditions respectively. Table 12 offers a sample interpretation of the Serenity Prayer which is used to open or close some mental health meetings and many twelve step meetings.

The Serenity Prayer

Key:

a) The line of the serenity prayer as it is spoken.
b) One interpretation offered by the authors.

---

a) God, grant me the serenity
b) God, give-me (directional) peace

---

a) to accept the things I cannot change
b) accept (body shift left) things me can't change

---

a) the courage to change the things I can
b) strength (body shift right) change things me can

---

a) and the wisdom to know the difference
b) (body shift neutral) wise know (head nod) point-left-right (two hands)

CONCLUSION: BEING RESTORED TO SANITY

My Creator, I am now willing that you should have all of me, the good and the bad. I pray that you will remove from me every single defect of character which stands in the way of my usefulness to you and my fellows. Grant me strength, as I go out from here, to do your bidding. (Seventh Step Prayer from the Big Book of AA, -p. 76)

Members of linguistic and cultural minorities present unique challenges to therapists who treat addictions, but education and awareness continue to improve the quality of care that is provided. Today there are treatment options and recovery programs that offer solutions to millions of addicts all over the world, in different languages, in different cultures – solutions that significantly improve the quality of life for many. Awareness of the linguistic and cultural diversity of the addict of who is deaf may help to restore an individual to sanity – a life that might otherwise be lost to the depths of hopelessness and despair caused by addiction.

The authors wish you the best of luck in your efforts to provide the opportunity for recovery to persons who are Deaf and hard of hearing. Feel free to contact us with your comments or questions:

Dr. Crone   amilto:ecrone@nationaldeafacademy.com
Dr. Goodman   cagood1@yahoo.com

REFERENCES

Easterbrooks, S.R. & Baker, S. (2002). *Language learning in children who are deaf and hard of hearing: Multiple pathways.* Boston: Allyn & Bacon.

Glickman, N. & Gulati, S. (Eds.) (2003). *Mental health care of deaf people: A Culturally Affirmative Approach.* Mahwah, NJ: Lawrence Erlbaum Assoc.

Humprhies, J. & Alcorn, B. (1995). *So you want to an interpreter? An introduction to sign language interpreting.* Amarillo, TX: H & H Pub.

Kannapel, 1993. Excerpt taken from a handout available from Dr. Crone at the National Deaf Academy.

Kemp, M. (1998). *Fundamentals of evaluating sign language programs: Checklists for program assessment.* San Diego: Dawn Sign Press.

Khantzian, E.J. (Dec. 2001). *Addiction: Disease, Symptom or Choice?* Counselor Magazine.

Knapp, S. & VandeCreek, L. (1998). *Privileged communications in the mental health professions.* NY: Van Nostrand Reinhold Col.

Jay, J. & Jay D. (2000). *Love first: A new approach to intervention for alcoholism and drug addiction.* Grosse Pointe Farms, MI: Hazelden.

Livingston, S. (1997). *Rethinking the education of deaf students: Theory and practice from a teacher's perspective.* Portsmouth, NH: Heinemann.

Lucas, D. & Valli, C. (1992). *Language contact in the American deaf community.* San Diego, CA: Academic Press.

Luetke-Stahlman, B. (1998). *Language issues in deaf education.* Hillsboro, OR: Butte.

Luetke-Stahlman, B. (1999). *Language across the curriculum when students are deaf or hard of hearing.* Hillsboro, OR: Butte.

Luetke-Stahlman, B. & Luckner, Jr. (1991). *Effectively educating students with hearing impairments.* White Plains, NY: Longman.

Schein, J.D. (1989). *At home among strangers.* Washington, DC: Gallaudet University Press.

Sussman, A. & Stewart, L. (Eds.) (1971). *Counseling of deaf people.* (p. 25). New York: New York University School of Education.

Tiebout, H.M. (1963; 2003). *Treating the causes of alcoholism.* Publication of Alcoholics Anonymous, The Grapevine.

Tresh, J. (1998; 2001). Guidelines for Sign Language Interpreters in Mental Health settings. National Deaf Academy.

U.S. Department of Education. (1998). *To assure the free appropriate public education of children with disabilities: 20th annual report to Congress on the implementation of the Individuals with Disabilities Education Act.* Washington, DC: US Government Printing Office.

APPENDIX A

Glossary of Terms

AA	Alcoholics Anonymous. Twelve step program based on abstinence from alcohol.
addiction	The use or abuse of alcohol or other drugs that results in problems physically, emotionally, mentally, spiritually, financially, or socially. It is considered a disease that manifests itself as a physical craving and mental obsession that requires a spiritual solution to achieve recovery.
contrived English	a form of manual communication which attempts to represent Standard English on the hands without regard to ASL parameters and features
deaf	the generic term used herein to refer to students who are either deaf, Deaf, or hard of hearing (noun)
Deaf	the cultural community of persons who are deaf or hard of hearing who use ASL as their primary mode of communication (noun)

English	standard written and spoken English
glossing	format used for notating the particular signs used; one English word is typically assigned to a sign or signed concept that may have numerous other meanings
hard of hearing	those whose hearing loss is not severe enough to warrant the label of "deaf" yet their ability to learn standard English is greatly impeded without the use of visual representation
individual	a one-on-one session between the client and therapist therapy
interpreter	a trained professional who is able to effectively facilitate communication between one or more parties who use ASL and those who use Standard English
language	a foundation for communication that adheres to an ascribed set of rules and structure; herein, English and ASL are the two languages being addressed
manual	any form of communication which entails the use of the hands to convey
communication	language and thought
manualism	an approach used to teach deaf and hard of hearing students based on the use of recognized signs and signed concepts
mode	a form of communication which attempts to follow a designated language, such as signed English and any of its contrived forms
NA	Narcotics Anonymous. A twelve step program designed for persons who are addicted to any form of drug, legal or illegal, including alcohol

oralism	an approach used to teach deaf and hard of hearing students based on maximizing aural and oral abilities and capabilities
PSE	Pidgin Signed English which attempts to incorporate many of the visual aspects of ASL in Standard English word order
recovery	Herin, the term refers to abstinence from the abusive use of alcohol and other drugs
signed English	Any of several communication modes which attempts to represent Standard English manually; it may include Conceptually Accurate Signed English (CASE), Seeing Essential English (SEE1), Signing Exact English (SEE2), or any other contrived form of English that is presented manually
sim-com	also referred to as simultaneous-communication; refers to signing and voicing at the same time
twelve-step program	Any of the programs that adhere to the principle that the solution to recovery is founded in changing one's actions which often happens before the mental change has been assimilated
transliterator	A trained professional who is able to facilitate effective communication between one or more parties who use a form of contrived signed English and Standard English
TTY/TDD	Teletypewriter/Telecommunications Device for the Deaf. A device used by the deaf like a telephone. An intermediary relay operator is used to connect the regular phone caller with the person who is using the TTY.
voicing	The interpreter verbalizes what the deaf client has signed to a hearing professional

APPENDIX B

Signs and Symptoms Checklist

Unusual Odors
Reeks of alcohol or marijuana residue
Chews gum or uses strong breath fresheners regularly
Abnormal Eye Dilations or Eye Contact
Eyes are overly dilated in well-lit areas
Unable to maintain appropriate eye contact during a conversation
Low Self-Esteem
Signs of grandiosity without appropriate follow-up
Insecure or unsure of him/herself
Changes in Appetite
Desire to eat is diminished or enhanced significantly
Loses or gains weight unexplainably
Legal Problems
Has received one or more DUI charges or accidents
Has legal problems (divorce, bill collectors, IRS, etc.)
Irritability and Aggressiveness
Defensive about drinking or other inappropriate behaviors

Hostile or aggressive toward others for no apparent reason
The Jekyll and Hyde Syndrome
Demonstrates erratic mood swings when drinking or using
Demonstrates erratic mood swings when not drinking or using
Financial Problems and Dishonesty
Has difficulty explaining the use or misuse of funds
Lies about where allocations have been appropriated
Employment
Does not have a job or changes jobs frequently
Has difficulty with relationships or responsibilities at work
Relationships
Problems with significant other
Affairs, improprieties, or indiscretions suspected
Self-Sufficiency and Isolation
Does not ask for help and even rejects help when offered
Often isolates in areas where s/he was once more amiable
Extremes
Extreme mood swings
Reacts, often irrationally, rather than responding to everyday occurrences
Interventions
One or more people have individually tried to help the person with his/her problem
Two or more people have jointly tried to discuss the person's problem with him/her

APPENDIX C

Resources for Intervention Support

Alcoholics Anonymous World Services. 1-212-870-3400.
www.alcholics-anonymous.org

Families Anonymous, Inc. 1-800-736-9805.
http://www.anukuesabibtniys, org

Larson, N..R., & Maddock, J .W. (2002). Violence and abuse in intimate relationships. *First Annual Conference on Sexuality and Intimacy: Conflict, Passion, and Power.* U.S. Journal Training, Inc. Las Vegas, NV: April 17-19, 2002.

Jay, J & Jay, D. (2000). *Love first: A new approach to intervention for alcoholism and drug addition.* Grosse Pointe Famrs, MI: Hazelden.

Myss, C. (1998). *Why people don't heal and how they can.* NY: Three Rivers Press.

PRIDE (Parents' Resource Institute for Drug Education). 1-800-241-7946. www.prideyouth.com

APPENDIX D

Consumer Bill of Rights

37.1.84.1. Rights of patients and residents. Each person who is a patient or resident in a hospital or other facility operated, funded, or licensed by the Department of Mental Health, Mental Retardation and Substance Abuse Services shall be assured his legal rights and care consistent with the basic human dignity insofar as it is within the reasonable capabilities and limitations of the Department or licensee and is consistent with sound therapeutic treatment. Except as may be limited on the basis of legal competence as adjudicated by a court of competent jurisdiction, each person admitted to a hospital or other facility operated, funded, or licensed by the Department shall:

(1)	Retain his legal rights as provided by state and federal law;
(2)	Receive prompt evaluation and treatment or training about which he is informed insofar as he is capable of understanding;
(3)	Be treated with dignity as a human being;

(4)	Not be the subject of experimental or investigational research without his prior written and informed consent or that of his guardian or committee;
(5)	Be afforded an opportunity to have access to consultation with a private physician at his own expense, and in the case of hazardous treatment or irreversible surgical procedures, have, upon request, an impartial review prior to implementation, except in the case of emergency procedures required for the preservation of his health;
(6)	Be treated under the least restrictive conditions consistent with his condition and not subjected to unnecessary physical restraint and isolation;
(7)	Be allowed to send and receive sealed letter mail;
(8)	Have access to his medical and mental records and be assured to their confidentiality but, notwithstanding other provisions of the law, such right shall be limited to access consistent with his condition and sound therapeutic treatment; and
(9)	Have the right to an impartial review of violations of the rights assured under this section and the right to access legal counsel.

APPENDIX E

Code of Ethics: Registry of Interpreter for the Deaf

1.	Interpreters/transliterators shall keep all assignment-related information strictly confidential.
2.	Interpreters/transliterators shall render the message faithfully, always conveying the spirit and intent of the speaker using language most readily understood by the person(s) whom they serve.
3.	Interpreters/transliterators shall not counsel, advise or interject personal opinions.
4.	Interpreters/transliterators shall accept assignments using discretion with regard to skill, setting, and the consumers involved.
5.	Interpreters/transliterators shall request compensation for services in a professional and judicious manner.
6.	Interpreters/transliterators shall function in a manner appropriate to the situation.

7.	Interpreters/transliterators shall strive to further knowledge and skills through participation in workshops, professional meetings, interaction with professional colleagues, and reading of current literature in the field.
8.	Interpreters/transliterators, by virtue of membership or certification by RID, Inc., shall strive to maintain high professional standards in compliance with the Code of Ethics.

APPENDIX F

The 12 Steps of AA and Suggested Interpretations

Key:

a)	The step as it is written.
b)	The glossed translation offered by the General Services Office of Alcoholics Anonymous, Box 459 Grand Central Station, New York NY 10163.
c)	An alternative glossed interpretation offered by the authors.

1. a)   We admitted we were powerless over alcohol – that our lives had become unmanageable.

1. b)   Admit alcohol strong than us. We can't control ourselves.

1. c)   We admit alcohol control can't; life before messed-up.

2. a)   We can to believe that a power greater than ourselves could restore us to sanity.

2. b) Believe "God", which is stronger than alcohol and us, can make our minds well again.

2. c) We believe true – power strong than ourselves help-me think clear again can.

3. a) We made a decision to turn our will and our lives over to the care of God, as we understood Him.

3. b) We decided to allow "God" to help our minds and lives. We pick "God" to believe.

3. c) We make decision do-do? Way, action, thinking surrender God – will!

4. a) We made a searching and fearless moral inventory of ourselves.

4. b) We made a list of things, good and bad, about ourselves. Not afraid, ashamed to make list.

4. c) We analyze (toward self) – wrong-wrong? put-down (list) fear shame none.

5. a) We admitted to God, ourselves, and another human being the exact nature of our wrongs.

5. b) Tell "God" and friends about list of good and bad about ourselves.

5. c) We admit (directional) to God, ourselves (spatial shift for "and") another person happen-happen before/past

6. a) We were entirely ready to have God remove all these defects of character.

6. b) Ready to allow "God" to change our bad habits.

6. c) We become ready allow God help me change wrong-wrong behaviors

7. a) We humbly asked Him to remove our shortcomings.

7. b)   Humbly ask "God" to help change our bad habits to good habits.

7. c)   We humbly ask (directional – Him) wrong-wrong behaviors remove

---

8. a)   We made a list of all persons we had harmed, and become willing to make amends to them all.

8. b)   Make a list of people we caused trouble, hurt. Become ready to tell them we are sorry.

8. c)   People hurt (spatial shift) insult before, make-list become willing meet-meet apologize A-L-L

9. a)   We made direct amends wherever possible, except when to do so would injure them or others.

9. b)   Tell people we are sorry, never do again. Make sure not to hurt those people or another person.

9. c)   People-meet-meet admit sorry finished. Suppose hurt again – withdraw stifle.

10. a)   We continued to take personal inventory and when we were wrong promptly admitted it.

10. b)   Keep on, continue looking at our good, bad ways, habits. Change bad ones.

10. c)   Everyday do-do? Inventory (self). Suppose wrong do-do? Admit sorry quick.

11. a)   We sought through prayer and meditation to improve our conscious contact with God as we understood Him, praying only for the knowledge of His will for us and the power to carry that out.

11. b)   We pray to "God" to help us talk with and understand His way and follow his way.

11. c)   Everyday pray (spatial shift "and") meditate for-for? Contact (God directional) for-for? Know His wish for us (spatial shift "and") strong follow (directional)

---

12. a) Having had a spiritual awakening as the result of these steps, we tried to carry this message to alcoholics, and practice these principles in all our affairs.

12. b) Spirit becomes better, improved because we follow these 12 Steps. We try to tell other alcoholics about 12 Steps. We want to follow 12 Steps everyday.

12. c) Now spirit-filled inspiration do-do? Help other alcoholics (spatial shift "and") follows steps all business.

Note: NA uses the same step with two modifications:

Step 1: Change the word "alcohol" to "addiction"
Step 2: Change the word "alcoholics" to "addicts"

APPENDIX G

The 12 Traditions of AA and Suggested Interpretations

Key:

a)   The tradition as it is written.

b)   The glossed translation offered by the general Services Office of Alcoholics Anonymous, Box 459 Grand Central Station, New York, NY 10163.

c)   An alternative glossed interpretation offered by the authors.

1. a)   Our common welfare should come first; personal recovery depends on AA unity.

1. b)   Taking care ourselves should come first, recovery individual depends on AA unity.

1. c)   Our common recovery/health priority; individual recover how? AA united.

2. a)   For our group purpose there is but one ultimate authority – a loving God as He may express Himself in our group conscience. Our leaders are but trusted servants; they do not govern.

2. b)   For our group purpose – there (is) only one (final) authority (loving) God (as) He maybe express Himself (in) our group conscience. Our leader trusted servants; they not govern.

2. c)   Groups have one boss – God. How know? Discuss-discuss agree-agree. Leader serve? Yes. Control? Not.

3. a)   The only requirement for AA membership is a desire to stop drinking.

3. b)   Only requirement for AA membership: desire (to) stop drinking.

3. c)   Become AA member only-one require – wish/desire drinking withdraw-from

4. a)   Each group should be autonomous except in matters affecting other groups or AA as a whole.

4. b)   Each group should be independent except for something affecting other groups or AA as a whole.

4. c)   Each group direct business itself. Influence other groups (spatial shift "or" AA general – Not!

5. a)   Each group has but one primary purpose – to carry the message to the alcoholic who still suffers.

5. b)   Each group has (but) one primary purpose – carry its message (to) alcoholic who still suffers.

5. c)   Groups AA – goal-one – help other alcoholics drinking suffering stop.

6. a)   An AA group ought never endorse, finance or lend the AA name to any related facilities or outside enterprise, lest problems of money, property, or prestige divert us from our primary purpose.

6. b)   Any AA group should never receive payment, rule money or lend AA's name (to) any related facility or outside business (enterprise) why? Problems – money, property, pride (prestige) separated us from our primary (important) purpose.

6. c)   AA name attach-to other hospital (spatial shift "or") business never! For-for? Problems money, property, ego pop-up. Goal off-the-point will.

7. a)   Every AA group ought to be fully self-supporting, declining outside contributions.

7. b)   Every AA group should be fully self-supporting, declining outside contributions.

7. c)   AA collect money from members; other people's money push-away

8. a)   Alcoholics Anonymous should remain forever non-professional, but our service centers may employ special workers.

8. b)   AA should remain forever non-professional; but our service centers can hire special workers.

8. c)   AA establish formal business not; (spatial shift "but") Hire special workers can.

9. a)   AA, as such, ought never be organized; but we may create service boards or committees directly responsible to those they serve.

9. b)   AA (itself) should never be organized; but maybe we create service boards or committees responsible (to) those they serve.

9. c)   AA itself same business not. Boards (spatial shift "and") committees resurrect can.

10. a) Alcoholics Anonymous has no opinion on outside issues; hence the AA name ought never be drawn into public controversy.

10. b)   AA has no opinion on outside issues; so name AA should never be involved into public controversy.

10. c)   AA involve with other business never. AA name stifle, not argue

11. a)   Our public relations policy based is based on attraction rather than promotion; we need always maintain anonymity at the level of press, radio

11. b)   Our public relations (PR) policy based on attraction rather than promotion; we need always maintain personal anonymity – (level of) press, radio, films.

11. c)   Advertise AA how? People look-at AA person – fascination-toward want. Brag-brag not. AA name relate newspaper radio movies closed-mouth.

12. a)   Anonymity is the spiritual foundation of all our Traditions, ever reminding us to place principles before personalities.

12. b)   Anonymity (is) spiritual foundation (of) all our Traditions, (ever) reminding us how principles first, 2nd – personalities.

12. c)   Privacy true spiritual foundation. Smash-in-forehead what? Steps important; people name not.

www.ingramcontent.com/pod-product-compliance
Lightning Source LLC
Chambersburg PA
CBHW061254280526
45784CB00002B/768